# TENDING the GARDEN

*A Blooming Bouquet of Quilts*

**Barb Adams**
and
**Alma Allen**
of
**BLACKBIRD DESIGNS**

# TENDING the GARDEN
## A Blooming Bouquet of Quilts

**Barb Adams**
*and*
**Alma Allen**
*of*
BLACKBIRD DESIGNS

**Editor:** Edie McGinnis
**Designer:** Bob Deck
**Photography:** Aaron T. Leimkuehler
**Illustration:** Eric Sears, Lisa Christensen and Alissa Christianson
**Technical Editor:** Jane Miller
**Photo Editor:** Jo Ann Groves

**Published by:**
Kansas City Star Books
1729 Grand Blvd.
Kansas City, Missouri, USA 64108

All rights reserved
Copyright © 2013 Barb Adams, Alma Allen and The Kansas City Star Co.

No part of this book may be reproduced, stored in a retrieval system, or transmitted in any form or by any means, electronic, mechanical, photocopying, recording or otherwise, without the prior consent of the publisher.

No finished quilts or other projects featured in this book can be produced or sold commercially without the permission of the author and publisher.

First edition, first printing
ISBN: 978-1-61169-092-7

Library of Congress Control Number: 2013938144

Printed in the United States of America by Walsworth Publishing Co., Marceline, MO

To order copies, call StarInfo at (816) 234-4242.

PickleDish.com
The Quilter's Home Page

# TABLE of CONTENTS

Introduction .................................... 5
Hand Appliqué Instructions ...................... 7
Missouri Daisy Quilt ............................ 9
Kansas Beauty Quilt ............................ 10
Missouri Daisy Supply List ..................... 12
Kansas Beauty Supply List ...................... 13
Plum Delicious Quilt ........................... 14
Plum Delicious Supply List ..................... 15
Block 1 ........................................ 16
Block 2 ........................................ 18
Block 3 ........................................ 20
Block 4 ........................................ 22
Block 5 ........................................ 24
Block 6 ........................................ 26
Finishing Instructions ......................... 28
Templates ...................................... 29
Tumbling Lily Quilt ............................ 52
My Heart is Yours Quilt ........................ 58
Sweet Remembrance Cross Stitch ................. 62
My Grandmother's Garden Cross Stitch ........... 66
Summer Home Hooked Rug ......................... 70
Shaker Sewing Box Hooked Rug ................... 76
Garden House Table or Bed Runner ............... 80
Vintage Blanket ................................ 92
Summer Stars Quilt ............................. 94

# ACKNOWLEDGEMENTS

This book would not have been possible without the contributions of many. Barb and I have worked with most of the following people for years. We choose to work with them because each offers a wonderful set of skills we couldn't do without. We offer a standing ovation to you all.

Many thanks go to Lauri Meyers and Sara Murray of the Vintage House. Their sweet home was the perfect location for our photography. Inspiration was everywhere, and it was the ideal backdrop for all of our projects.

Not only did Sandy Williams hook our *Summer Home* rug in a week's time, but also her attention to color and texture enhances any design. Her shop, American Whatever, is a great resource in our community.

Jeanne Zyck's quilting graces all of our projects, and this time she appliquéd and pieced several projects for us, too. We can always count on her craftsmanship to make our projects wonderful.

Many hours of time must be devoted to bring projects to completion. One person who is always willing to help is Barb's mother, Leona Adams. We couldn't get much done without her.

Pat Ryan stitched both cross stitch pieces included in our book. We're not sure exactly how many pieces she has stitched for us over time, but we are certain of the perfection of her stitches.

Computer skills are necessary to illustrate some of our ideas. Lisa Christensen gave us our digital quilt, *Plum Delicious*, using scans of our fabric and a few clicks of the mouse. She didn't even need a needle or thread!

Alissa Christianson charts our cross stitch patterns. It takes talent to show the design in chart form, and with Alissa's skills, we now have a clear and accurate picture of where the stitches need to be placed.

Bob Deck's cover and page design has given us the compelling look we always strive to achieve. His choice of fonts, color and arrangement of the text and pictures makes us want to linger on each page.

Aaron T. Leimkuehler's photographic ability gives us the pictures we long to see. Each angle is exactly right.

Photos always need a bit of color correction, and sometimes a thread has to be removed digitally. Thanks to Jo Ann Groves, what you see on the page is how the quilt should look.

We need someone to check our supply lists and cutting instructions so we are sure our patterns are mathematically correct. Jane Miller does all this and more. She makes all of our lives easier.

None of this would be possible without the help of our editor. Edie McGinnis edits all of our publications for good reason. Her careful attention to detail helps us write clear and accurate instructions. She organizes the project and helps move the book along to the end product we desire. She is exactly who we need!

# INTRODUCTION

Put your work gloves away and don't bother to unearth the hoe or the rake. There are no bulbs or seeds to buy, and there will be no weeding as you tend to this garden. You won't even end up with sore muscles as you work on the lovely bouquet of quilts and projects blooming on the following pages.

It's always a surprise to see what a change in color can do for a quilt, so we made our featured quilt in three different colorways. By using a darker background and a subtle color palette, Barb's quilt, *Missouri Daisy*, takes on the look of an autumn garden. The snowy, white flowers sparkle, and make the quilt a show-stopper in any room. You can see Barb's quilt on pages 8 and 9.

I used sweet, soft traditional colors when I made my quilt, *Kansas Beauty*. The quilt, with its clean, simple lines fairly begs to be folded back so one can slip underneath and take a small nap. You can see the quilt on pages 10 and 11.

*Plum Delicious* on page 12, is our third color way. It has been made from our fabric line, *Field Notes* for Moda Fabrics. One of the background prints looks like a botanical, bird study guide. The garden-inspired textures of this quilt add comfort and softness to a room. Combine this quilt with textures, such as wicker and sun-bleached finishes, to bring the outdoors inside.

If you could see all the quilts that Barb and I have made over the years, you could tell we love the look of large, floral appliqué. The quilts, just like a fresh bouquet of flowers, look at home no matter where they are displayed. But sometimes we like to take a break from appliqué and whip up something dramatic, yet simple. If that's the mood you are in, take a look at page 94. *Summer Stars* with its simple cream and red colorway looks like the essence of summer.

A couple of hooked pieces have been added for those who love rug hooking like we do. It doesn't appear anyone has been tending the hooked rug garden on pages 74 and 75. The enormous flowering vines have grown around the house. Large folk art butterflies visit, looking for a bit of nectar.

The handmade Shaker box shown on pages 77 and 78 is one of our favorite finds of the year. Stephanie Elmer from Springhill, Kansas, makes these boxes in her woodworking shop. The special lip in the box lid provides a space for a circular hooked or cross stitched piece to slip into. We have topped our Shaker box with a small container of hooked flowers. We've included her information so you can add one of these great boxes to your collection, too.

The cross stitch sampler on page 66 was done in memory of my grandmother. I added her full name and place of residence along the bottom and her year of birth over the roof. An alphabet and numbers are charted so you can stitch this piece in memory of someone you hold dear.

Barb has included her secret recipe for giving a vintage crochet coverlet new life. We have been using these as accent pieces on the bed, table and even over the sofa. No longer do these wonderful pieces have to be hidden in the closet because of age spots and stains. Bring them out and dye them in great new colors.

Grab your needle and thread and let's begin to sow a creative seed. Lush fabric flowers on a quilt, small cross stitched flowers on linen, or hooked wool flowers growing around a house require no water or weeding. Their only need is a bit of quiet, creative and peaceful time. Come with us as we tend our gardens.

*-Alma Allen*

# HAND APPLIQUÉ

- Make templates of the appliqué shapes using freezer paper or plastic template material. Do not add any seam allowance to these shapes.

- If using plastic, trace around the templates on the right side of your fabric. Use a marking pencil that will be easy to see. This drawn line indicates your seam line. To cut reversed pieces, flip the plastic template over and trace the reversed shape to the right side of the fabric. If using freezer paper, first trace the shapes onto the dull side of the paper. Iron the paper templates, shiny side down, onto the right side of the fabric. Trace around the template. Peel the paper template away carefully, as it can be reused. For a reversed piece, trace on the shiny side of the paper.

- After the seam line has been drawn on the right side of the fabric, cut out the shapes, adding a $\frac{1}{8}$" - $\frac{1}{4}$" seam allowance.

- Fold the background fabric in half vertically and horizontally. Finger press the folds. Open the fabric.

- To help achieve placement of the design, refer to the block diagram located with the templates. A one-inch grid was added to each diagram to indicate position for the pieces. If you look closely at each quilt block, you will notice each is unique. The pieces were placed on the block in a whimsical fashion.

- Center the design on the background block using the fold lines and placement diagram as a guide.

- Baste the shapes into place on the background block with a glue stick or appliqué pins. Larger shapes require basting stitches to hold the shapes in place securely.

- Use thread that matches your appliqué piece, not the background. Use a two-ply, cotton thread that is 50-60 weight.

- Cut the thread length about 12" - 15". Longer lengths of thread may become worn and break as you stitch.

- For concave curves (curves that go in) clip to the seam line, then turn under the seam allowance. This will allow the fabric to lie flat. Convex curves (or curves that go out) do not require clipping.

- Sew the pieces that will be covered by another piece first. For example, sew the stems first. Next, sew the flower or leaf that covers the end of the stem.

- Using the point and edge of your needle, turn under the fabric on the drawn seam line and appliqué the shape to the background fabric. Try to achieve about 7-9 stitches per inch.

# MISSOURI DAISY

**Project Size - 84" x 84"    Finished Block Size - 28"**

# KANSAS BEAUTY

Project Size - 84" x 84"   Finished Block Size - 28"

# MISSOURI DAISY

*Design by* **Barb Adams**
*Appliqué by* **Barb Adams**
*Quilted by* **Jeanne Zyck**

### SUPPLY LIST

The fabric numbers are from the collection of **Cinnamon Spice** by Blackbird Designs for Moda Fabrics.

**For the background:**

- 7 ¼ yds. tan print (2703-14)

**For the appliqué pieces:**

- ¼ yd. each of 4 different ivory prints for the flowers
- Fat quarter each of 5 different purple prints and plaids for the baskets and flowers
- ½ yd. of a different purple print
- ⅔ yd. each of 7 different dark green and brown prints and plaids for the stems and leaves
- 1 bottle of Rit dye - tan
- 10 yds. of white rick rack
- ¼" & ½" Clover bias tape makers

# KANSAS BEAUTY

*Design by* **Alma Allen**
*Appliqué by* **Jeanne Zyck**
*Quilted by* **Jeanne Zyck**

## SUPPLY LIST

The fabric numbers are from the collection of **Cinnamon Spice** by Blackbird Designs for Moda Fabrics.

### For the background:

- 4 ⅛ yds. of a light cream and pink print (2702-11)
- 3 ⅓ yds. of a light cream and pink stripe (2706-11)

### For the appliqué pieces:

- Fat quarter each of 2 different blue prints for the baskets
- ¾ yd. each of 3 different green prints for the leaves (2704-23, 2704-13, & 2701-13)
- ¾ yd. of a khaki print for the leaves (2703-14)
- ¾ yd. of a green check for the stems
- Fat quarter each of 3 different red prints for the flowers (2700-12, 2705-12, & 2704-12)
- 1 yd. of a different red print for the flowers and binding (2706-12)
- Fat quarter each of 3 different pink prints for the flowers (2703-15, 2704-15, & 2701-15)
- ¼" & ½" Clover bias tape makers

13

# PLUM DELICIOUS

Project Size - 84" x 84"   Finished Block Size - 28"

*Design by* Barb Adams
*Graphic Design by* Lisa Christensen

## SUPPLY LIST

The fabric numbers are from the collection of **Field Notes** by Blackbird Designs for Moda Fabrics.

### For the background:

- 4 ⅛ yds. of a light cream print (2716-11)
- 3 ⅓ yds. of a light botanical print (2710-11)

### For the appliqué pieces:

- Fat quarter of a grey print for 3 baskets (2712-13)
- Fat quarter of a grey stripe for 2 baskets (2718-13)
- Fat quarter each of 2 different blue prints for leaves (2712-18 & 2716-18)
- 1 yd. each of 2 different green prints for the leaves and stems (2717-17 & 2714-17)
- 2 yds. of a green print for the leaves and stems (2715-17)
- Fat quarter each of 5 heather/plum prints for the flowers (2718-15, 2717-16, 2711-16, 2716-15 & 2712-16)
- Fat quarter of a yellow print for the flower centers (2713-12)
- ⅞ yd. of a plum print for the binding
- ¼" & ½" Clover bias tape makers

## BLOCK ONE

Cutting measurements include a ¼" seam allowance.

- Cut 1 - 28 ½" square from a background print.
- You will find the placement diagram and templates needed for this block on pages 30 - 31. Refer to the photo for color placement.
- Make 1 ⅓ yd. of ½" bias tape for the larger flower stems.
- Make 1 yd. of ¼" bias tape for the smaller flower stems.
- Cut out the shapes, adding a ⅛" - ¼" seam allowance. Refer to the diagram on page 30 and baste the pieces in place on the background block.
- Appliqué the pieces in place.

## BLOCK TWO

Cutting measurements include a ¼" seam allowance.

- Cut 1 - 28 ½" square from a background print.
- You will find the placement diagram and templates needed for this block on pages 32 - 35. Refer to the photo for color placement.
- Make 1 ¾ yds. of ½" bias tape for the larger flower stems.
- Make ⅔ yd. of ¼" bias tape for the smaller flower stems.
- Cut out the shapes, adding a ⅛" - ¼" seam allowance. Refer to the diagram on page 32 and baste the pieces in place on the background block.
- Appliqué the pieces in place.

## BLOCK THREE

Cutting measurements include a ¼" seam allowance.

- Cut 1 - 28 ½" square from a background print.

- You will find the placement diagram and templates needed for this block on pages 36 - 40. Refer to the photo for color placement.

- Make ½ yd. of ½" bias tape for the larger flower stems.

- Make 2 ¼ yds. of ¼" bias tape for the smaller flower stems.

- Cut out the shapes, adding a ⅛" - ¼" seam allowance. Refer to the diagram on page 36 and baste the pieces in place on the background block.

- Appliqué the pieces in place.

## BLOCK FOUR

Cutting measurements include a ¼" seam allowance.

- Cut 1 - 28 ½" square from a background print.

- You will find the placement diagram and templates needed for this block on pages 41 - 44. Refer to the photo for color placement.

- Make 1 ½ yds. of ½" bias tape for the larger flower stems.

- Make 1 ¾ yds. of ¼" bias tape for the smaller flower stems.

- Cut out the shapes, adding a ⅛" - ¼" seam allowance. Refer to the diagram on page 41 and baste the pieces in place on the background block.

- Appliqué the pieces in place.

## BLOCK FIVE

Cutting measurements include a ¼" seam allowance.

- Cut 1 - 28 ½" square from a background print.

- You will find the placement diagram and templates needed for this block on pages 45 - 48. Refer to the photo for color placement.

- Make ½ yd. of ½" bias tape for the larger flower stems.

- Make 1 ¾ yds. of ¼" bias tape for the smaller flower stems.

- Cut out the shapes, adding a ⅛" - ¼" seam allowance. Refer to the diagram on page 45 and baste the pieces in place on the background block.

- Appliqué the pieces in place.

25

## BLOCK SIX

Cutting measurements include a ¼" seam allowance.

- Cut 1 - 28 ½" square from a background print.
- You will find the placement diagram and templates needed for this block on pages 49 - 51. Refer to the photo for color placement.
- Cut out the shapes, adding a ⅛" - ¼" seam allowance. Refer to the diagram on page 49 and baste the pieces in place on the background block.
- Appliqué the pieces in place.
- Make 4 of these blocks.

27

# FINISHING

## Kansas Beauty and Plum Delicious
- Refer to the pictures on pages 10 and 14. Sew the blocks together to form the quilt top.

## Missouri Daisy
- Refer to the picture on page 9 and sew the blocks together.

## Rick Rack Binding
- Quilt the quilt before sewing the rick rack in place. Baste the rick rack onto the edge of the right side of the quilt and continue all the way around. Add a bit of extra rick rack as you baste around each corner. Clip if needed. When you come back to the place you began, fold the raw rick rack edges over into the seam allowance and overlap the rick rack a bit.

- Cut bias strips 1 ½" wide. Sew them together until you have 8 ½ yds. Use this strip for your binding. Sew the binding in place with the right side of the strip, facing the right side of the quilt top. The rick rack will be sandwiched between the quilt top and the binding. Fold the binding over to the back of the quilt, turn under a seam allowance and whip stitch in place.

## DYEING INSTRUCTIONS

- Combine 8 cups of warm water with ½ cup of liquid Rit tan dye. Add 4 tablespoons of salt. Mix well.

- Add 10 yds. of rick rack into the dye bath for approximately 15 minutes. Mix the rick rack in the solution to make sure all parts of the rick rack are dyed evenly.

- Remove the trim from the dye bath when you are pleased with the results. The trim will dry lighter. Rinse until the water runs clear and allow it to air dry. Press if needed.

# BLOCK ONE

Each square = 1 inch

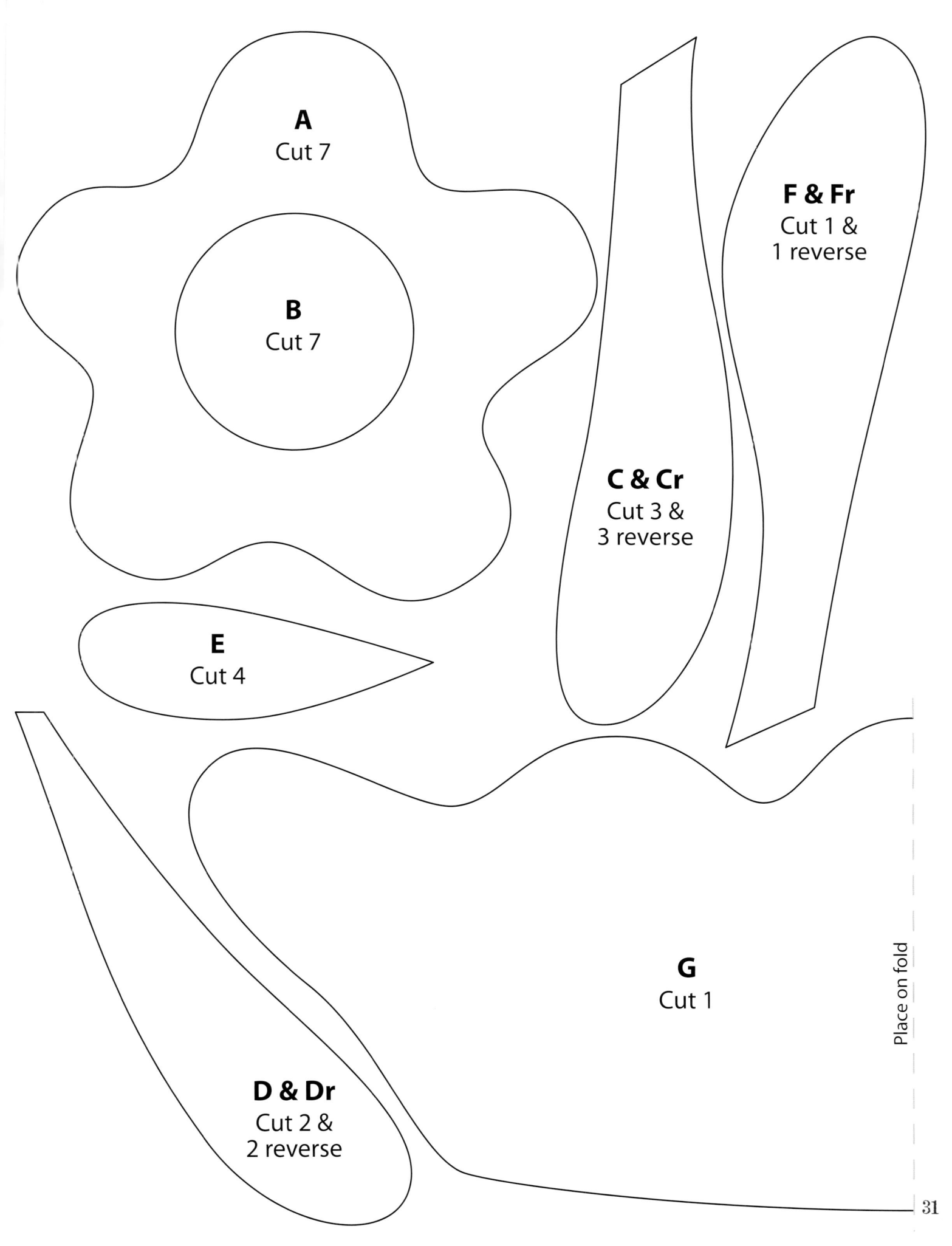

# BLOCK TWO

Each square = 1 inch

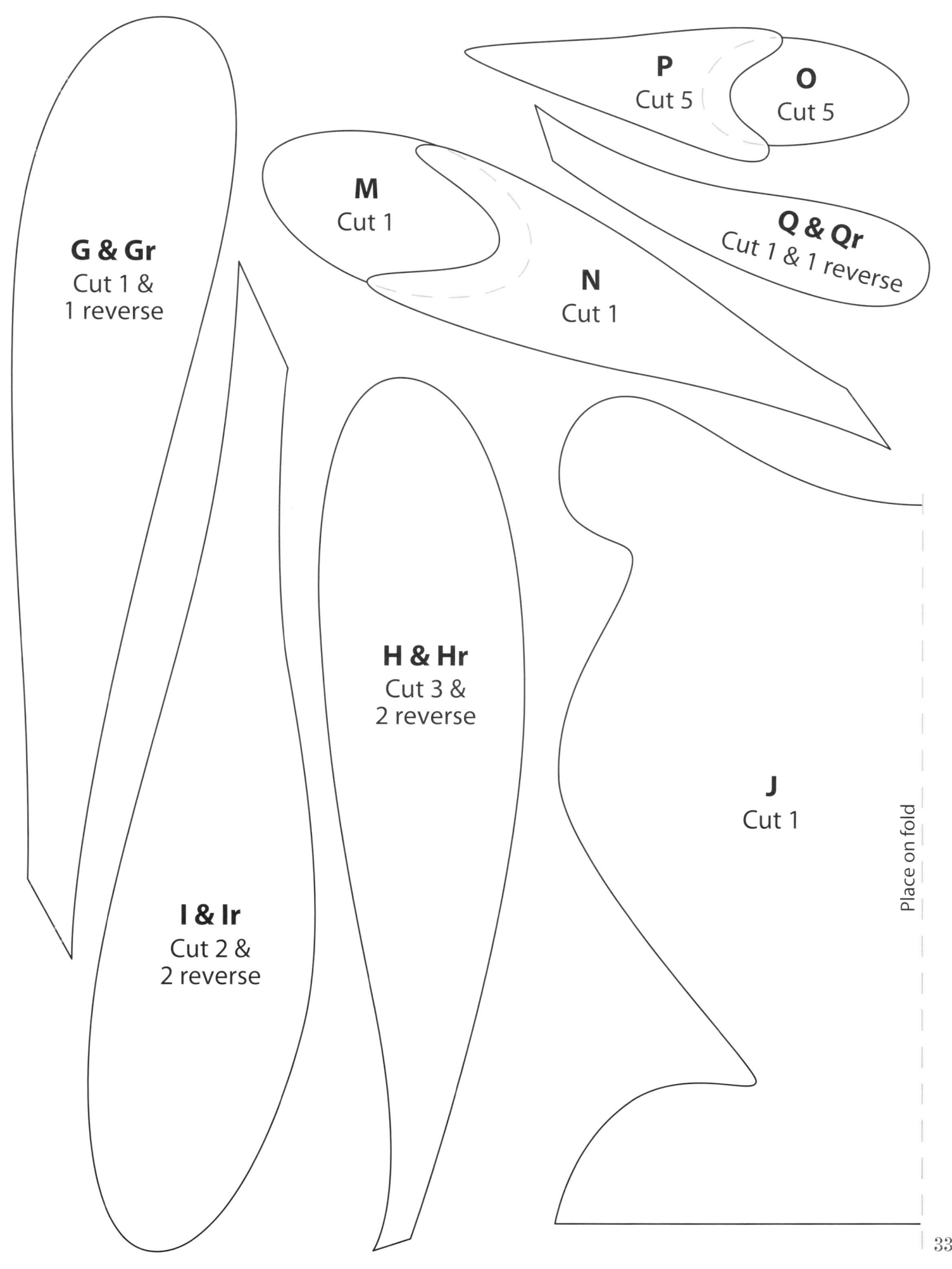

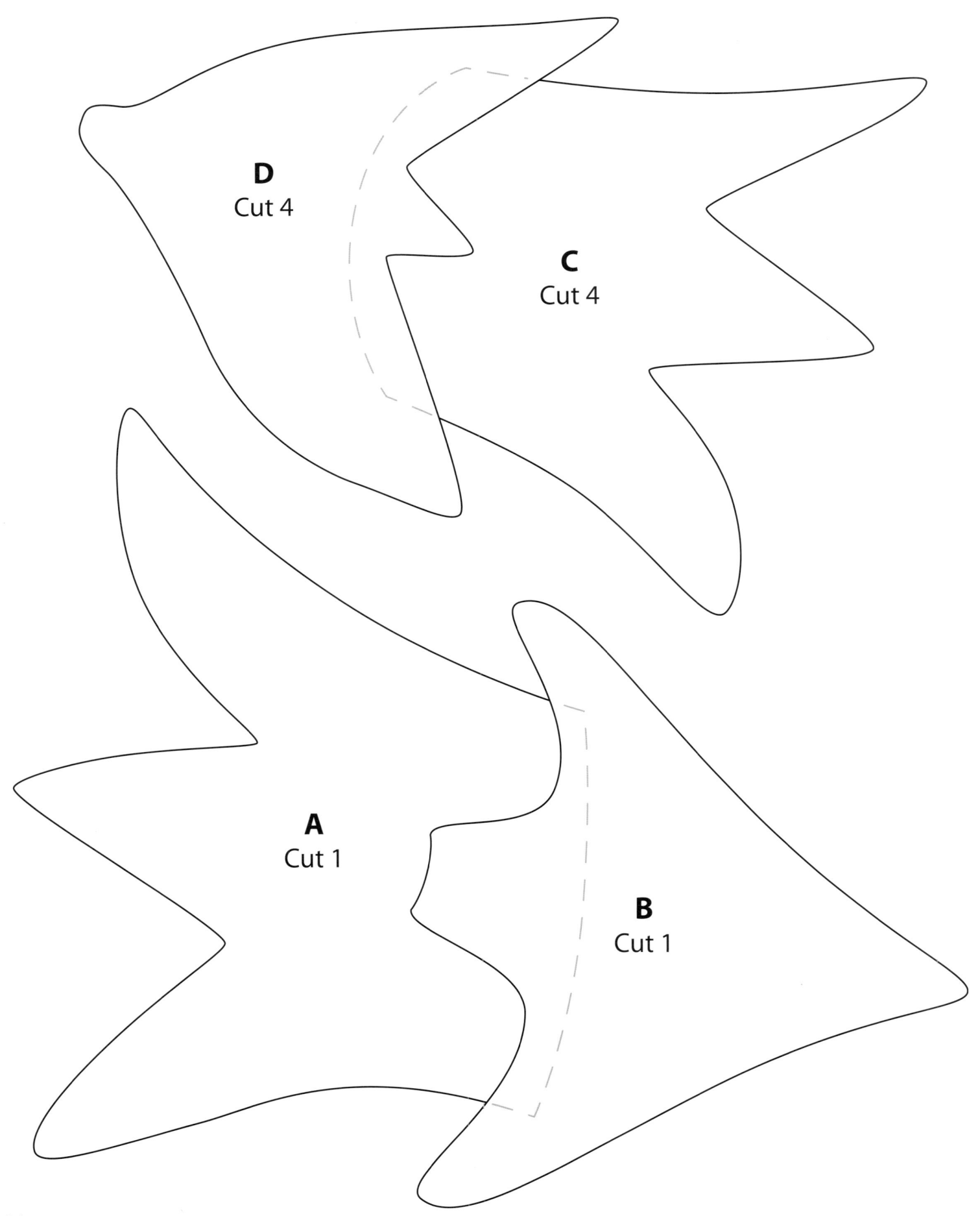

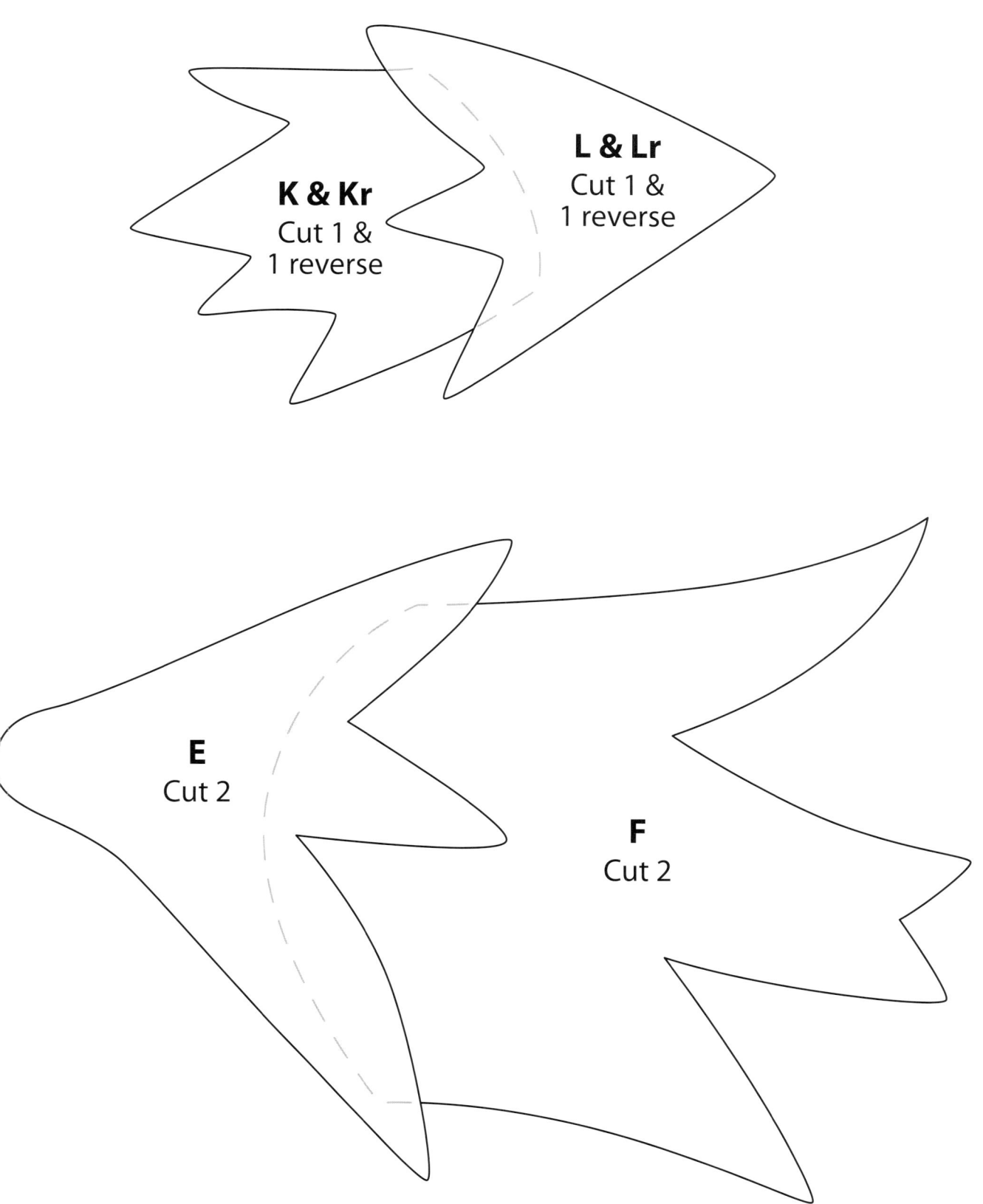

# BLOCK THREE

Each square = 1 inch

**A**
Cut 1

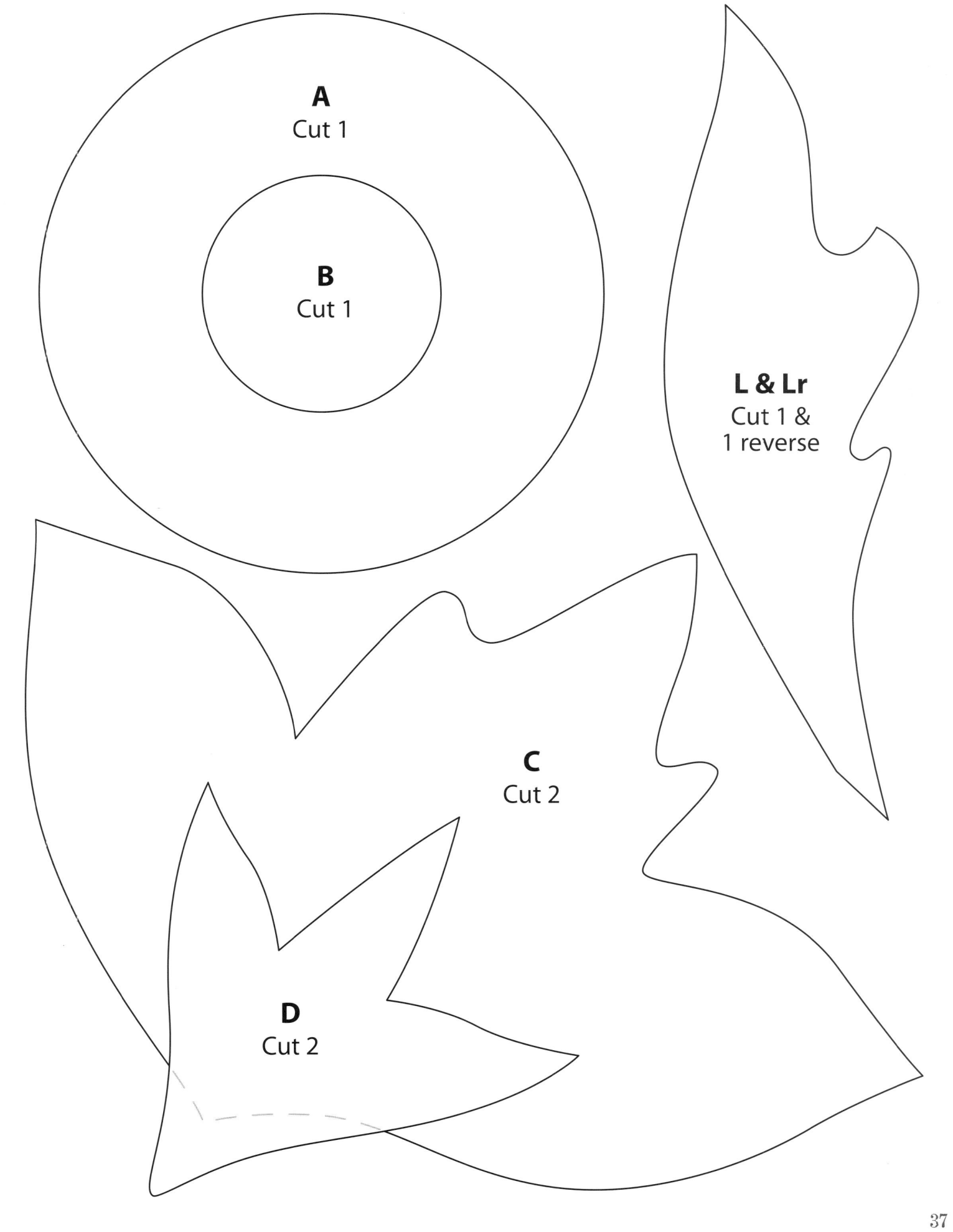

**B**
Cut 1

**L & Lr**
Cut 1 &
1 reverse

**C**
Cut 2

**D**
Cut 2

37

**S & Sr**
Cut 1 &
1 reverse

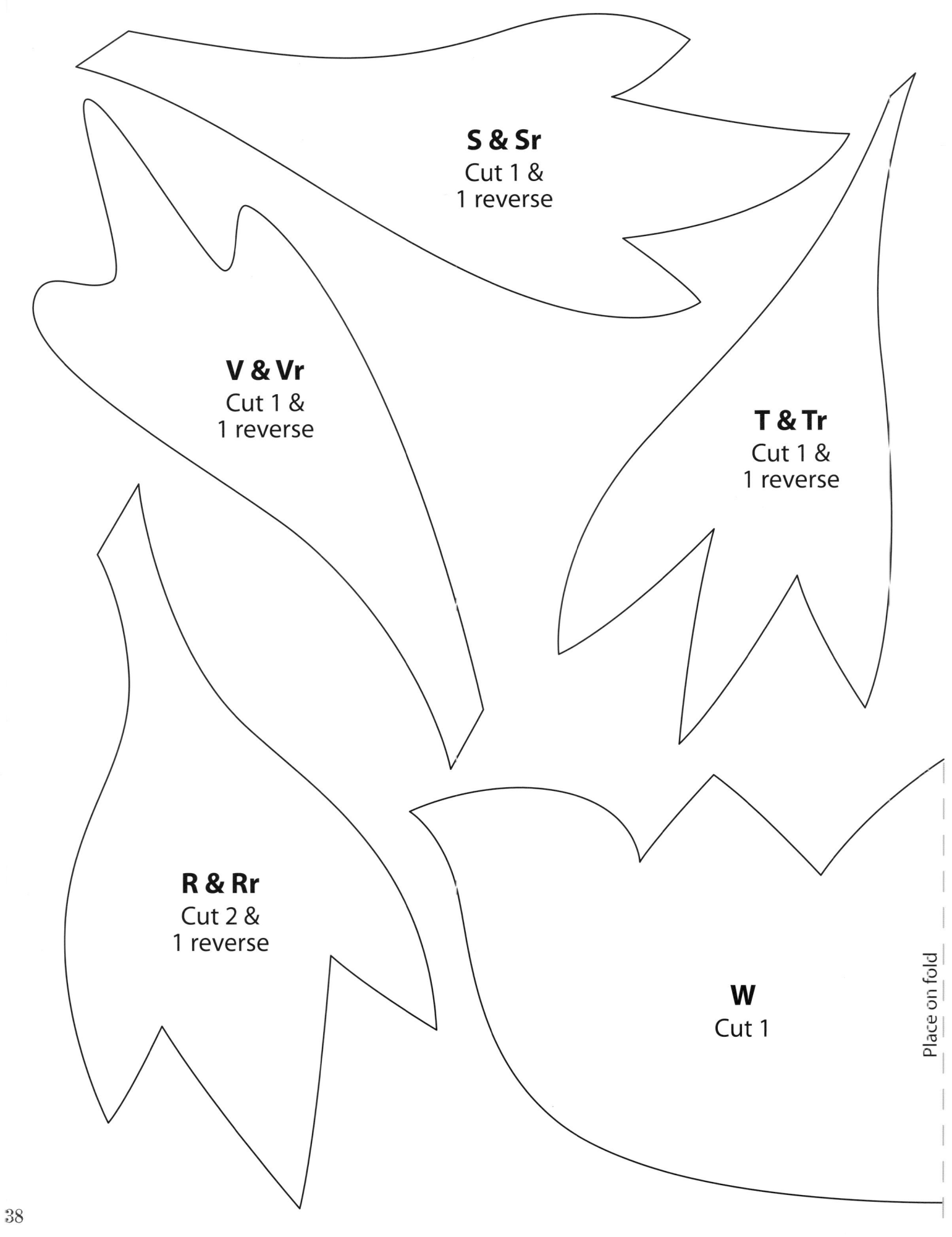

**V & Vr**
Cut 1 &
1 reverse

**T & Tr**
Cut 1 &
1 reverse

**R & Rr**
Cut 2 &
1 reverse

**W**
Cut 1

Place on fold

**P** Cut 2

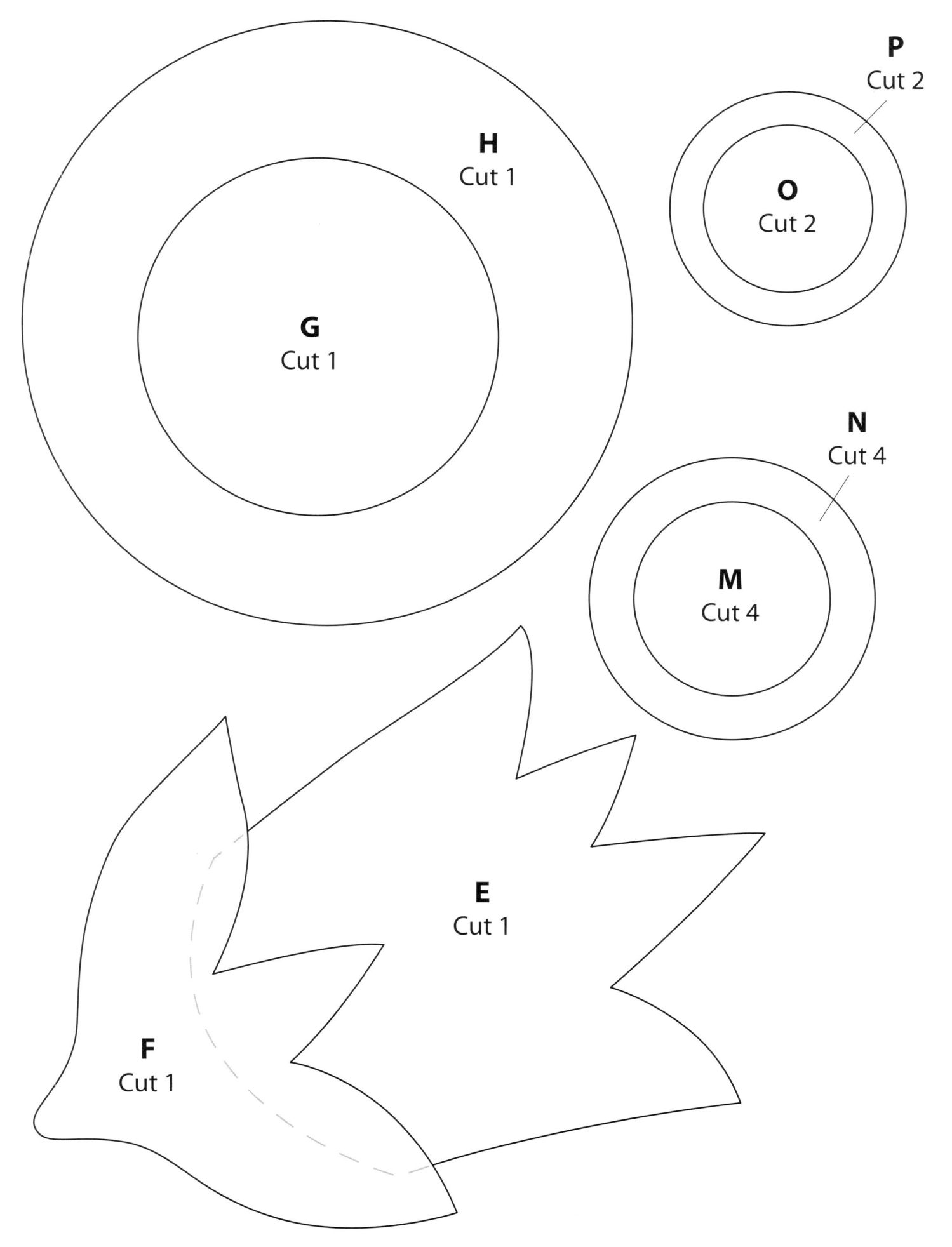

**O** Cut 2

**H** Cut 1

**G** Cut 1

**N** Cut 4

**M** Cut 4

**E** Cut 1

**F** Cut 1

**J**
Cut 2

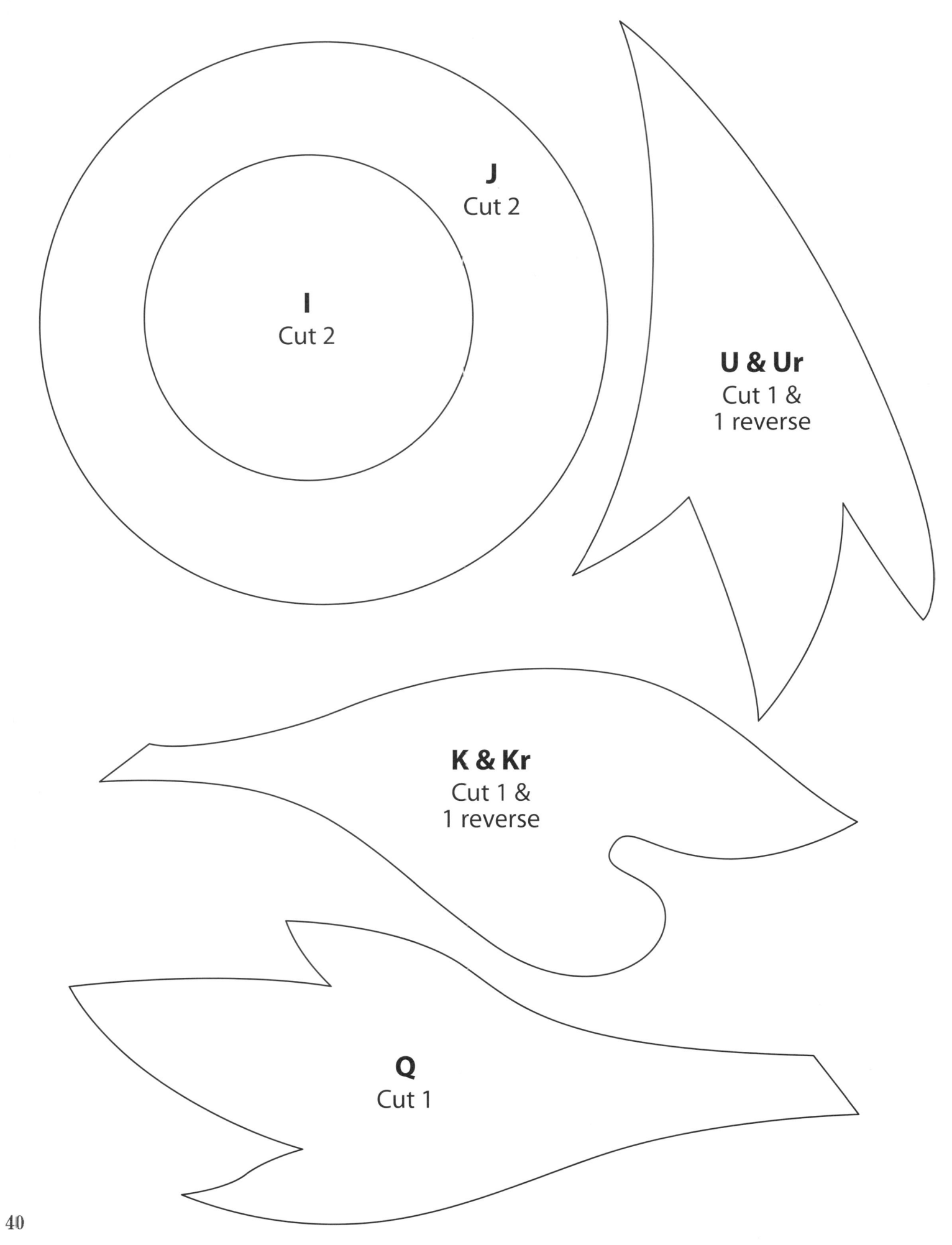

**I**
Cut 2

**U & Ur**
Cut 1 &
1 reverse

**K & Kr**
Cut 1 &
1 reverse

**Q**
Cut 1

# BLOCK FOUR

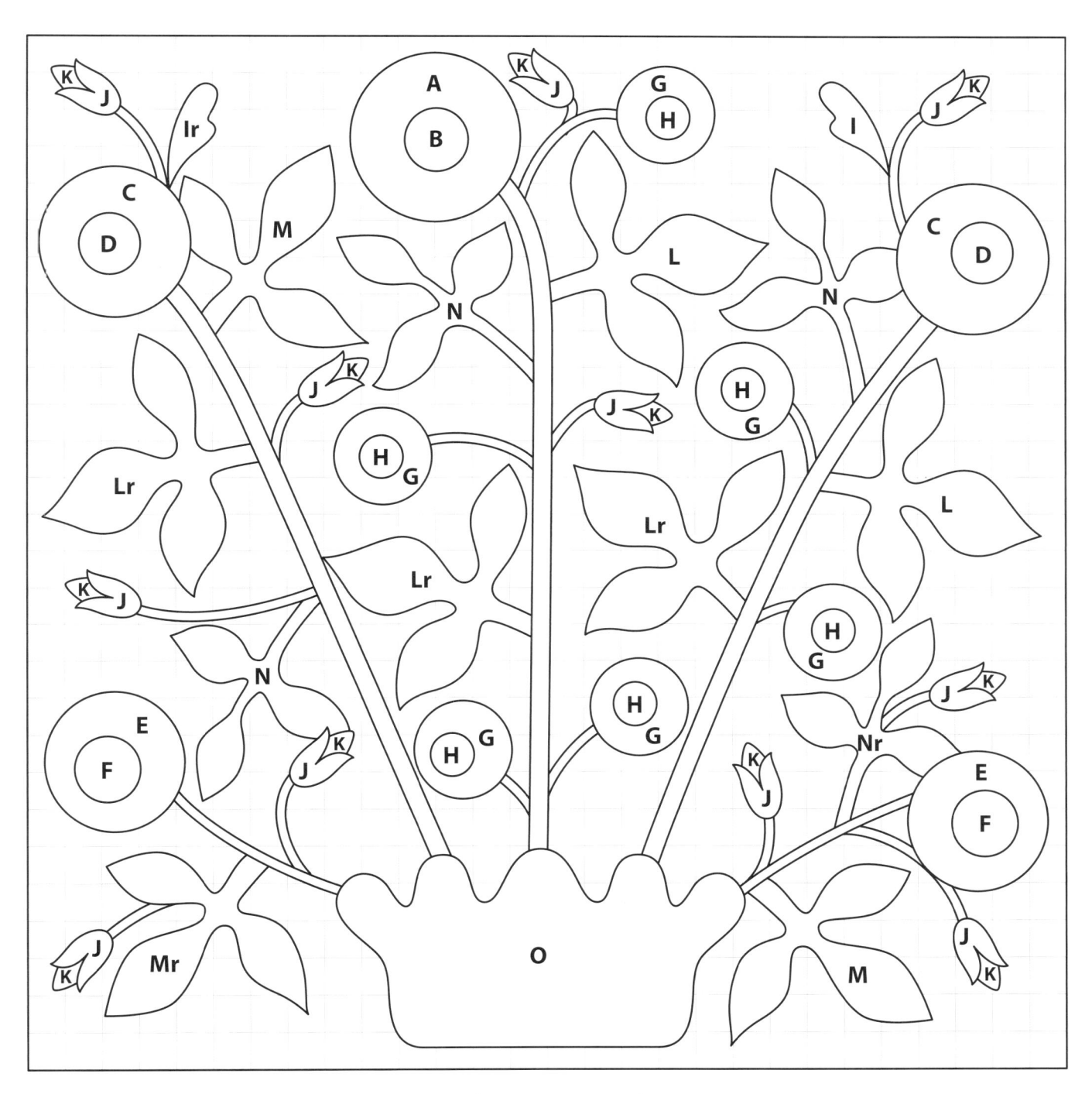

Each square = 1 inch

41

**A**
Cut 1

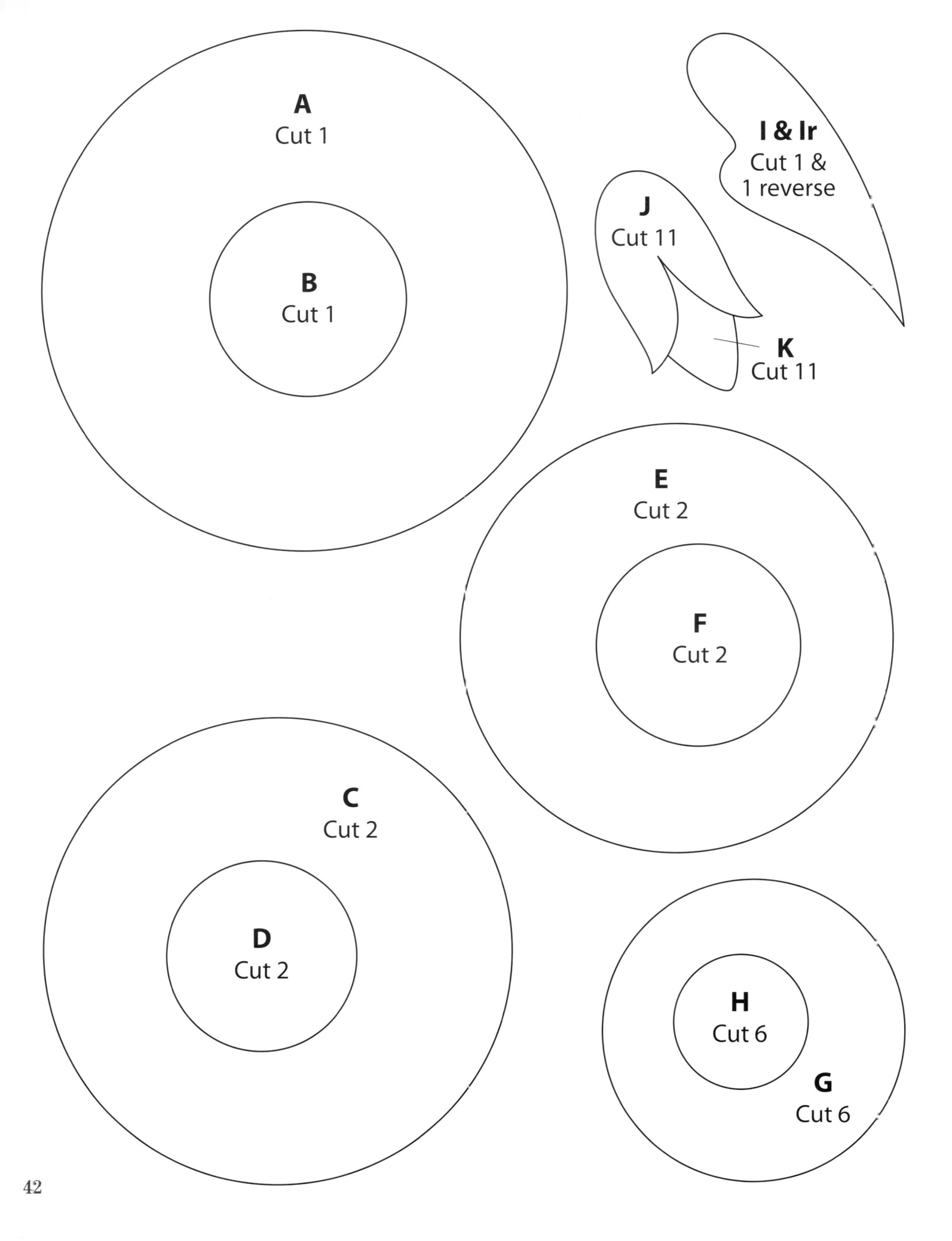

**B**
Cut 1

**I & Ir**
Cut 1 &
1 reverse

**J**
Cut 11

**K**
Cut 11

**E**
Cut 2

**F**
Cut 2

**C**
Cut 2

**D**
Cut 2

**H**
Cut 6

**G**
Cut 6

**N & Nr**
Cut 3 &
1 reverse

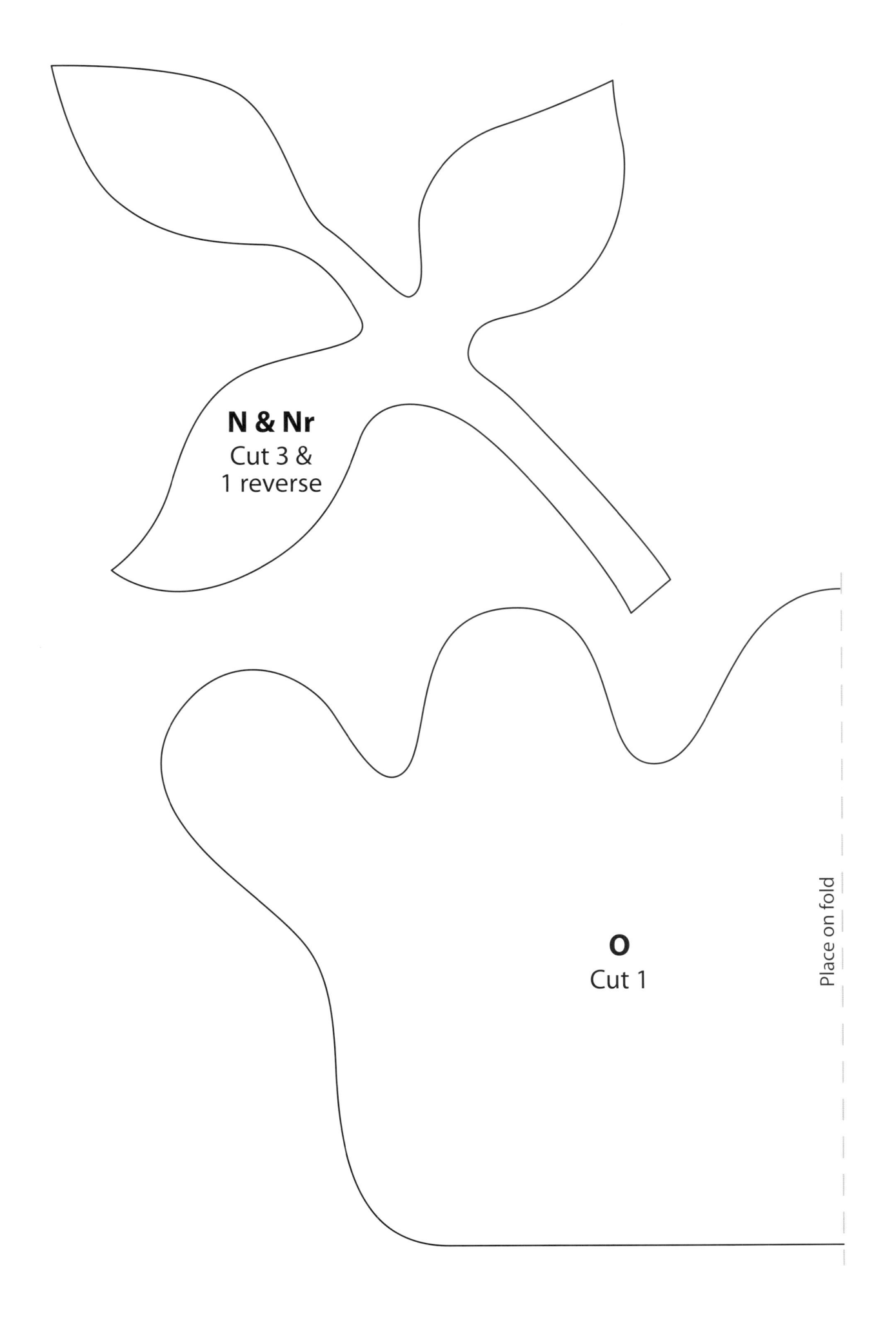

**O**
Cut 1

Place on fold

43

**L & Lr**
Cut 2 &
3 reverse

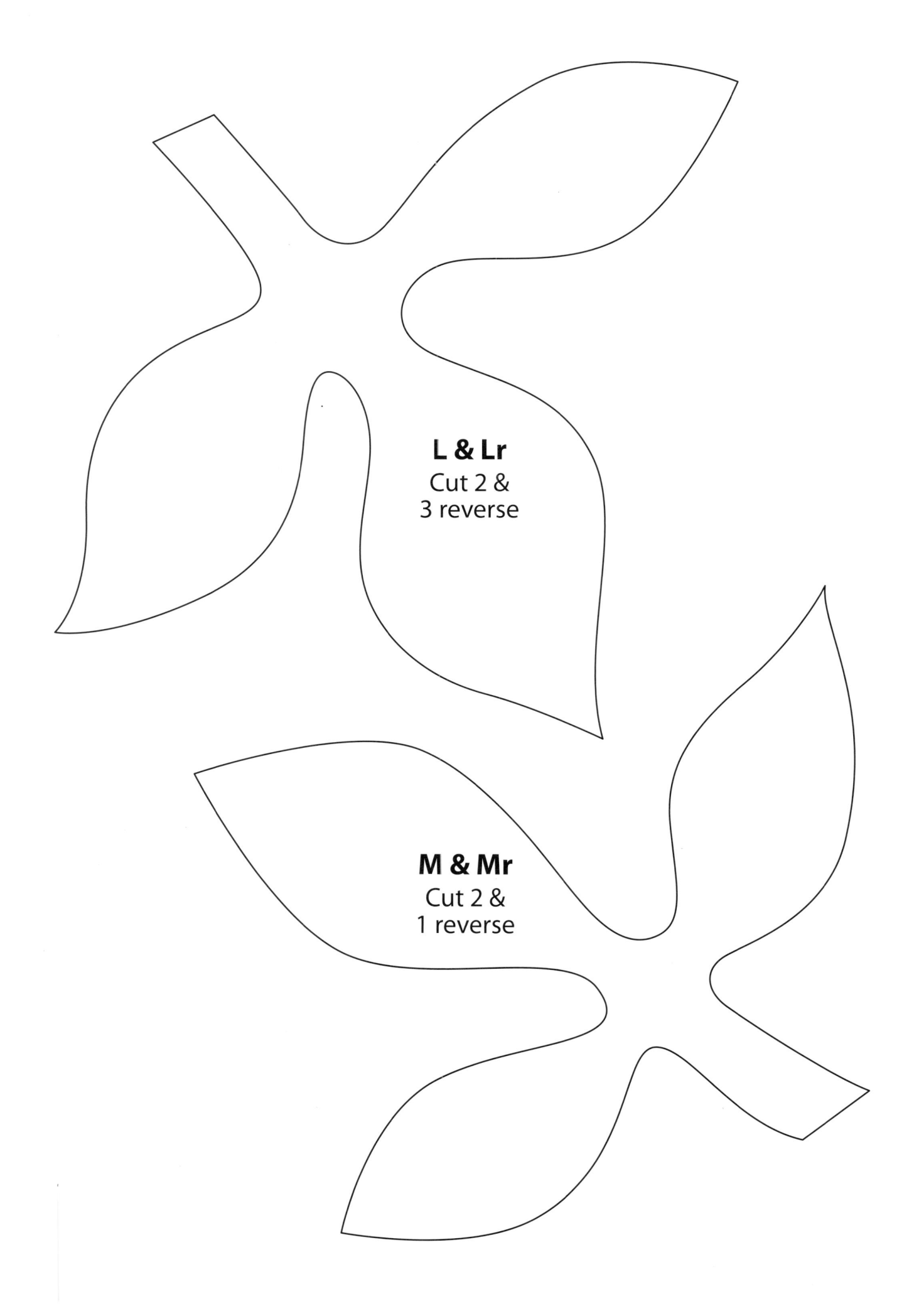

**M & Mr**
Cut 2 &
1 reverse

# BLOCK FIVE

Each square = 1 inch

45

**C**
Cut 2

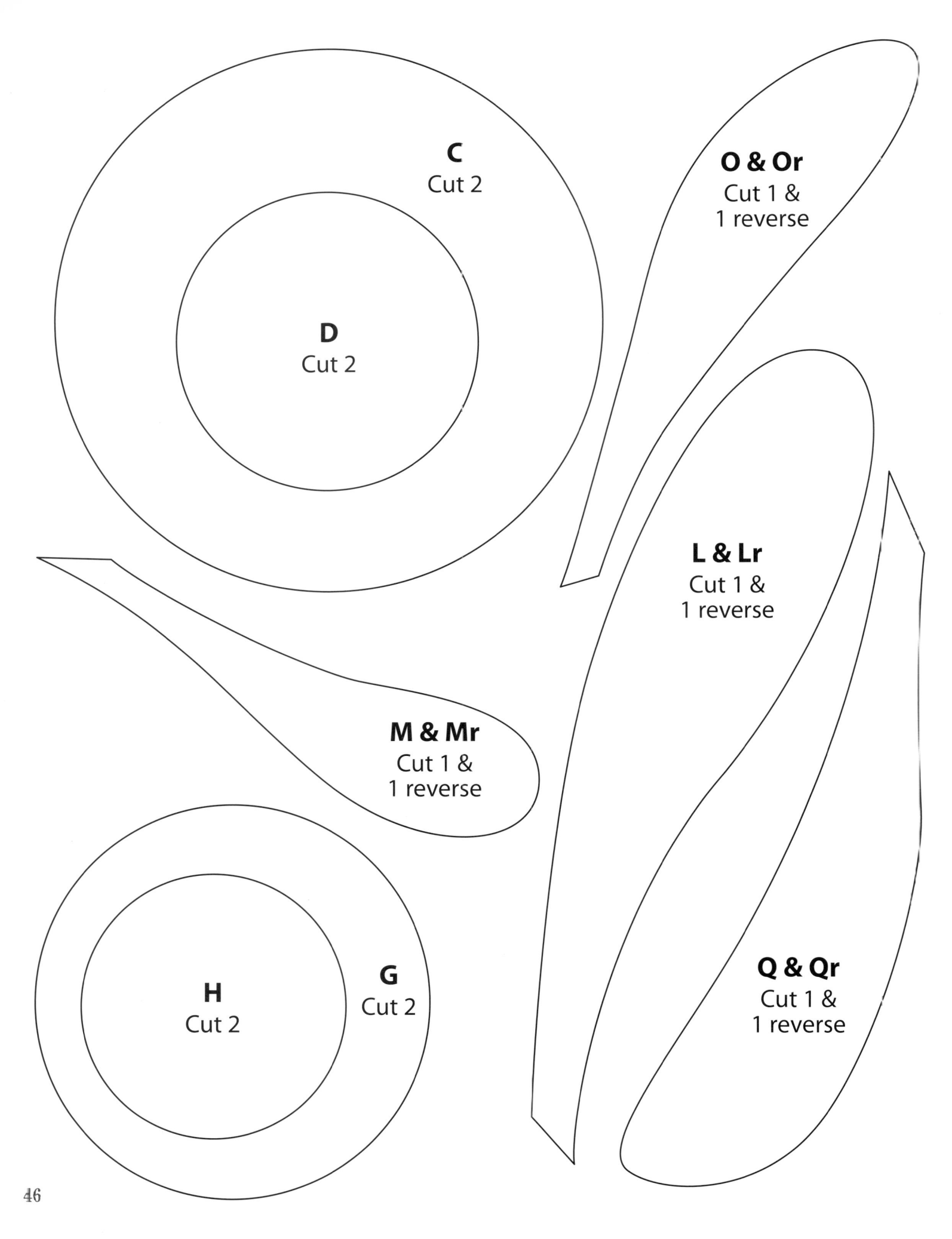

**D**
Cut 2

**O & Or**
Cut 1 &
1 reverse

**L & Lr**
Cut 1 &
1 reverse

**M & Mr**
Cut 1 &
1 reverse

**H**
Cut 2

**G**
Cut 2

**Q & Qr**
Cut 1 &
1 reverse

**K & Kr**
Cut 2 &
2 reverse

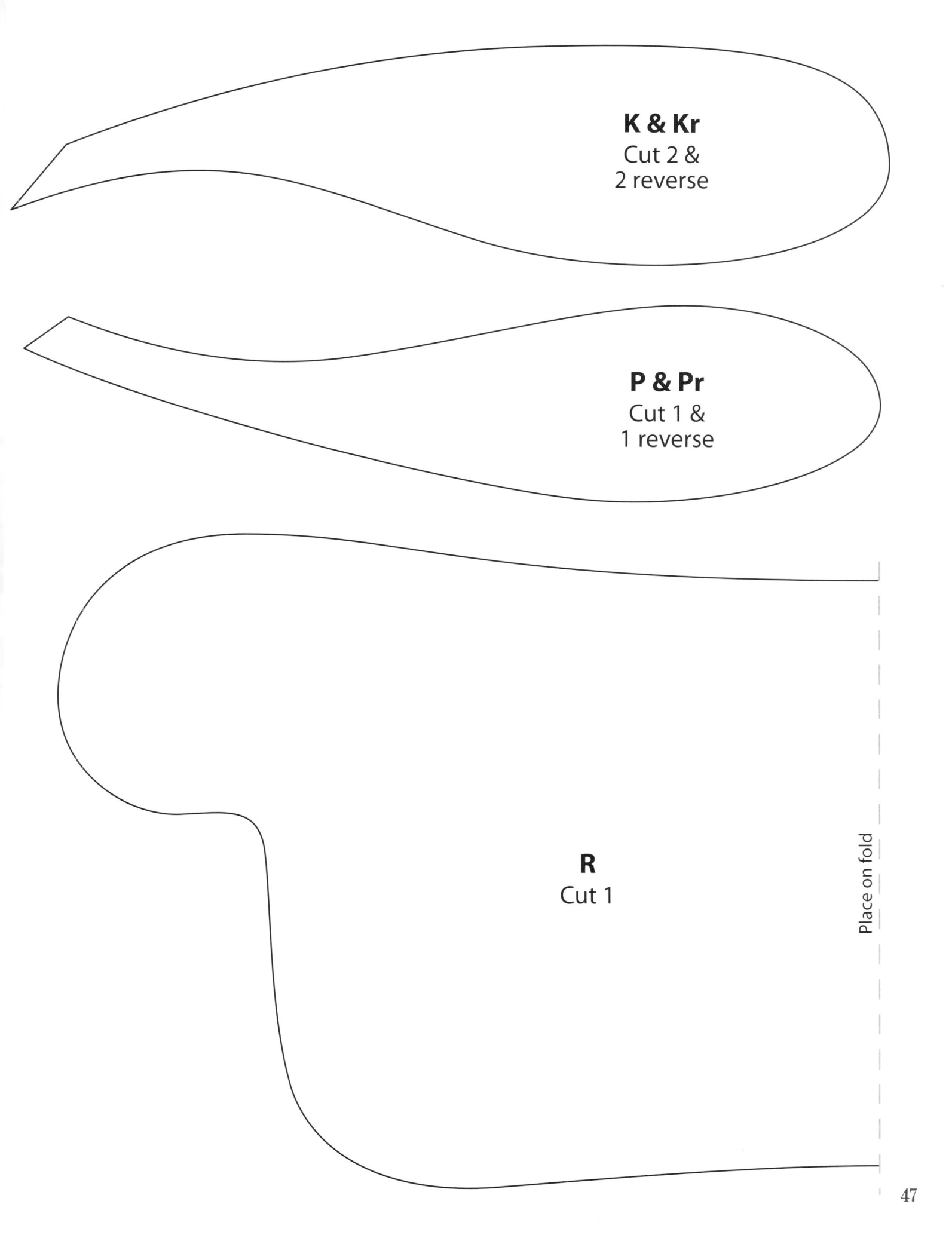

**P & Pr**
Cut 1 &
1 reverse

**R**
Cut 1

Place on fold

**A**
Cut 1

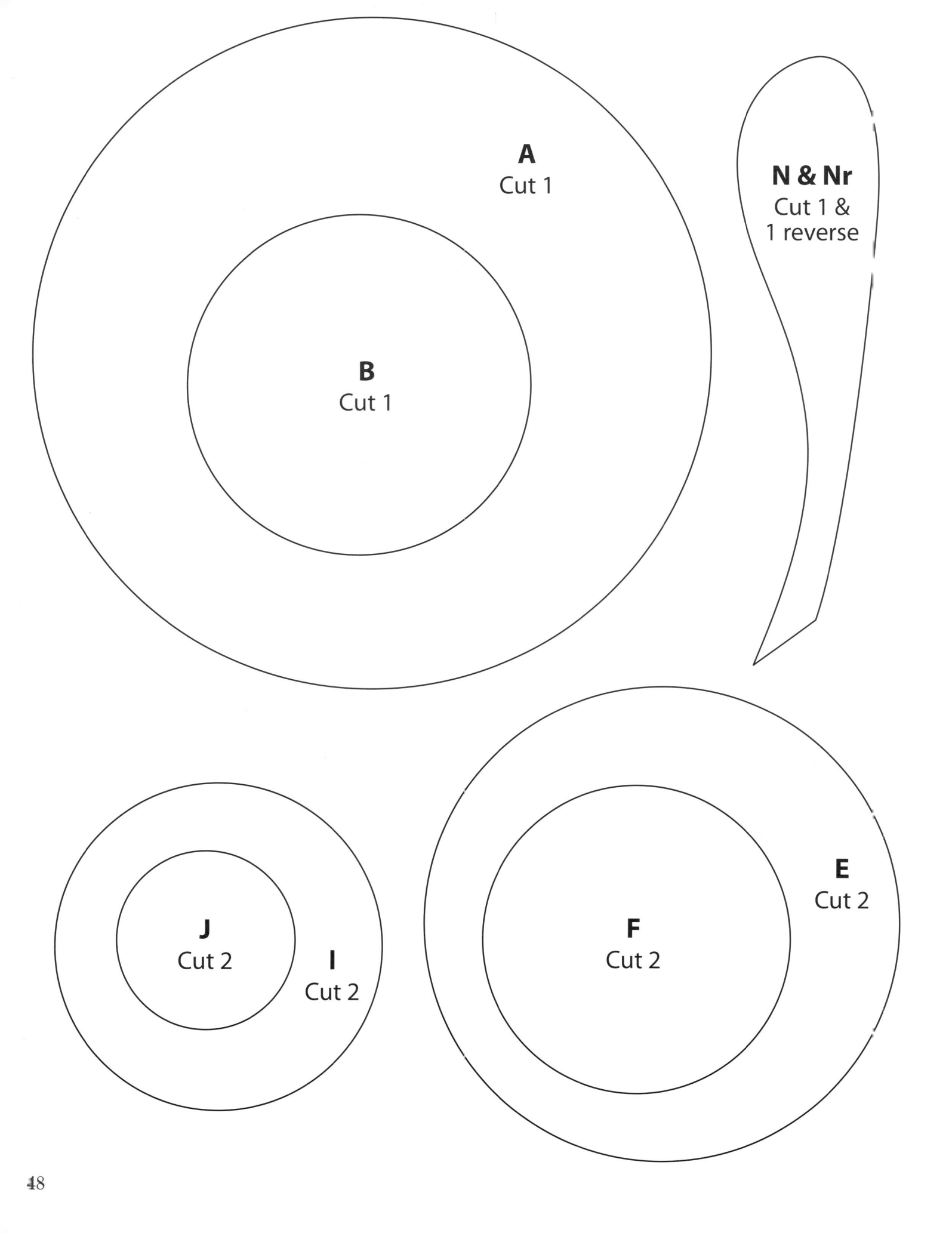

**B**
Cut 1

**N & Nr**
Cut 1 &
1 reverse

**J**
Cut 2

**I**
Cut 2

**F**
Cut 2

**E**
Cut 2

# BLOCK SIX

Each square = 1 inch

Join template here

Join template here

**Leaf**
Cut 16

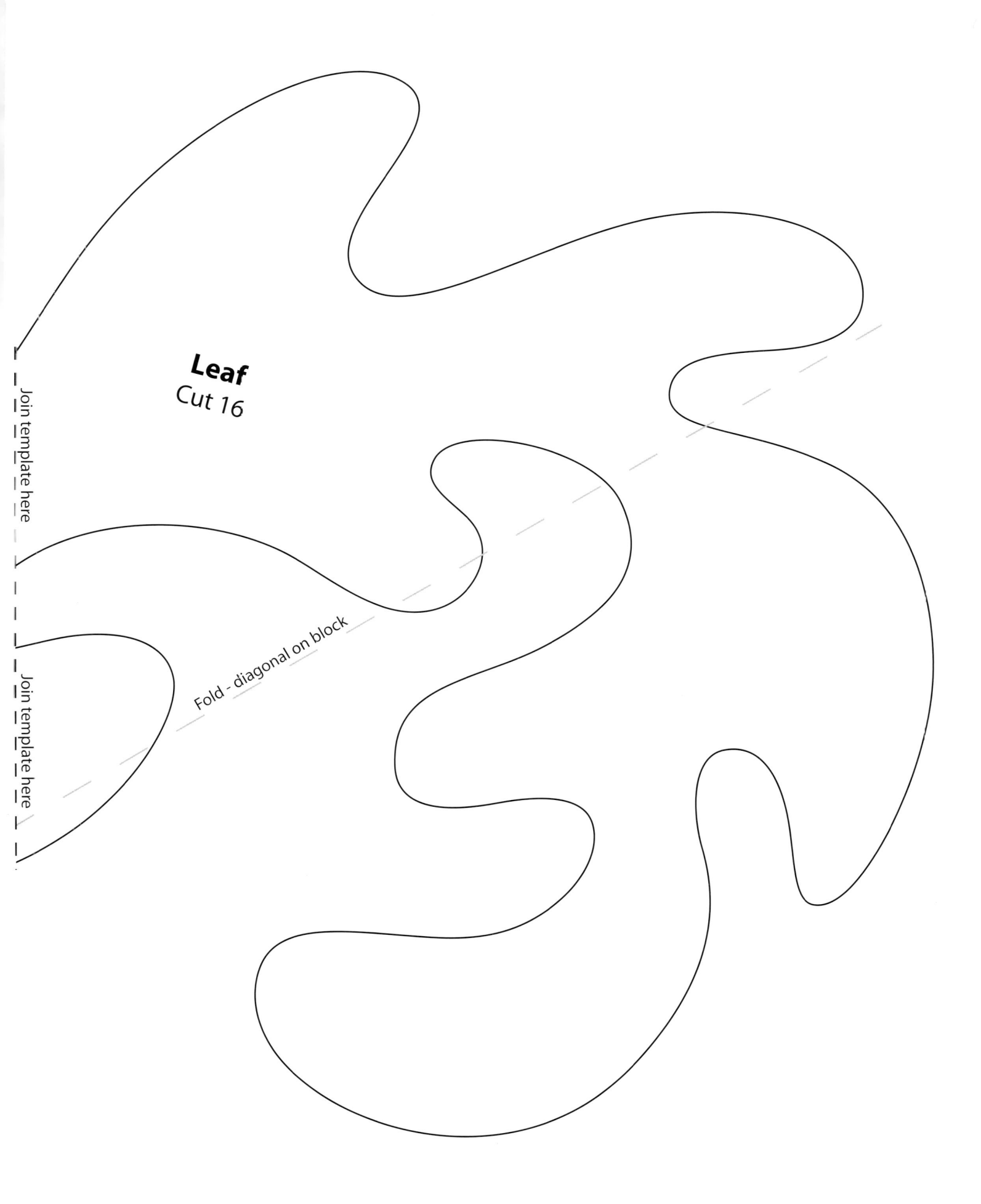

Fold - diagonal on block

Join template here

Join template here

51

# TUMBLING LILY

Project Size - 65" x 65"   Finished Block Size - 20"

*Design by* **Barb Adams**
*Appliqué by* **Jeanne Zyck**
*Quilting by* **Jeanne Zyck**

## SUPPLY LIST

The fabric numbers are from the collection of **Cinnamon Spice** by Blackbird Designs for Moda Fabrics.

- ¾ yd. each of 6 different light prints for the backgrounds (2702-11, 2706-11 and 4 additional prints)
- 1 ¼ yds. of a red print for the ruffle (2701-12)
- ½ yd. for the binding

### For the appliqué pieces:

- ⅓ yd. each of 5 different red prints (2701-12, 2705-12, 2706-12, 2704-12 and 2700-12)
- ⅓ yd. each of 3 different pink prints (2701-15, 2703-15 and 2704-15)
- ⅓ yd. each of 6 different tan prints (2704-24, 2702-13, 2703-14, 2704-14, 2700-14 and 2706-14)
- ⅓ yd. each of 5 different green prints (2703-13, 2704-13, 2704-23, 2700-13 and 2701-13)
- ½" Clover bias tape maker

## INSTRUCTIONS

Cutting measurements include a ¼" seam allowance.

- Cut 4 - 10 ½" squares from the background prints. Sew the 4 - 10 ½" squares together to make one large 20" block.
- You will find the placement diagram and templates needed for this block on pages 56 - 57. Refer to the photo for color placement.
- Make 6 yds. of ½" bias tape for the flower stems. This is enough for all of the blocks.
- Cut out the shapes, adding ⅛" - ¼" seam allowance. Refer to the diagram on page 56 and baste the pieces in place on the background.
- Repeat the above steps to make 9 blocks.
- Sew the 9 blocks together to make the quilt top.

*Instructions continue on page 55.*

54

# BORDER INSTRUCTIONS

- Cut 48 - 3 ⅜" squares from the assorted red and pink prints.
- Cut 48 - 3 ⅜" squares from the assorted light prints.
- Draw a diagonal line down the center of the lighter square. Refer to the diagram below. Place one lighter square atop a red square with right sides facing. Sew ¼" on either side of the drawn line.

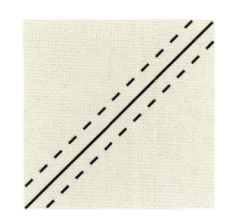

- Cut the block apart on the drawn line. The result will be two half-square triangles. Press each block open. Repeat for 80 half-square triangles.

- Refer to the illustration below. Sew two half-square triangles together into units as illustrated below.

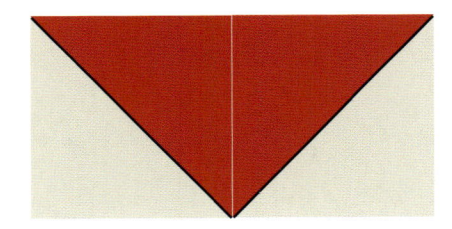

- Sew 4 strips of 12 units each. Sew one strip to each side of the quilt top.
- Cut 4 - 3" squares from a red print. Sew one square to each end of the two remaining strips.
- Sew one strip to the top and one to the bottom of the quilt top.

# THE RUFFLED EDGING

- Quilt the quilt before adding the ruffle.
- Cut 16 yds. of 2 ½" bias strips. Sew the strips together. Press in half lengthwise. Gather the ruffle. Baste in place along the edge of the quilt top.
- Cut 8 - 1 ¾" x 45" strips. Sew the strips together. This piece will be the binding. Sew the strip on, sandwiching the ruffle between the quilt top and the binding. Turn the binding towards the back, turn under the seam allowance and whip stitch in place.

# TUMBLING LILY PLACEMENT GUIDE *and* TEMPLATES

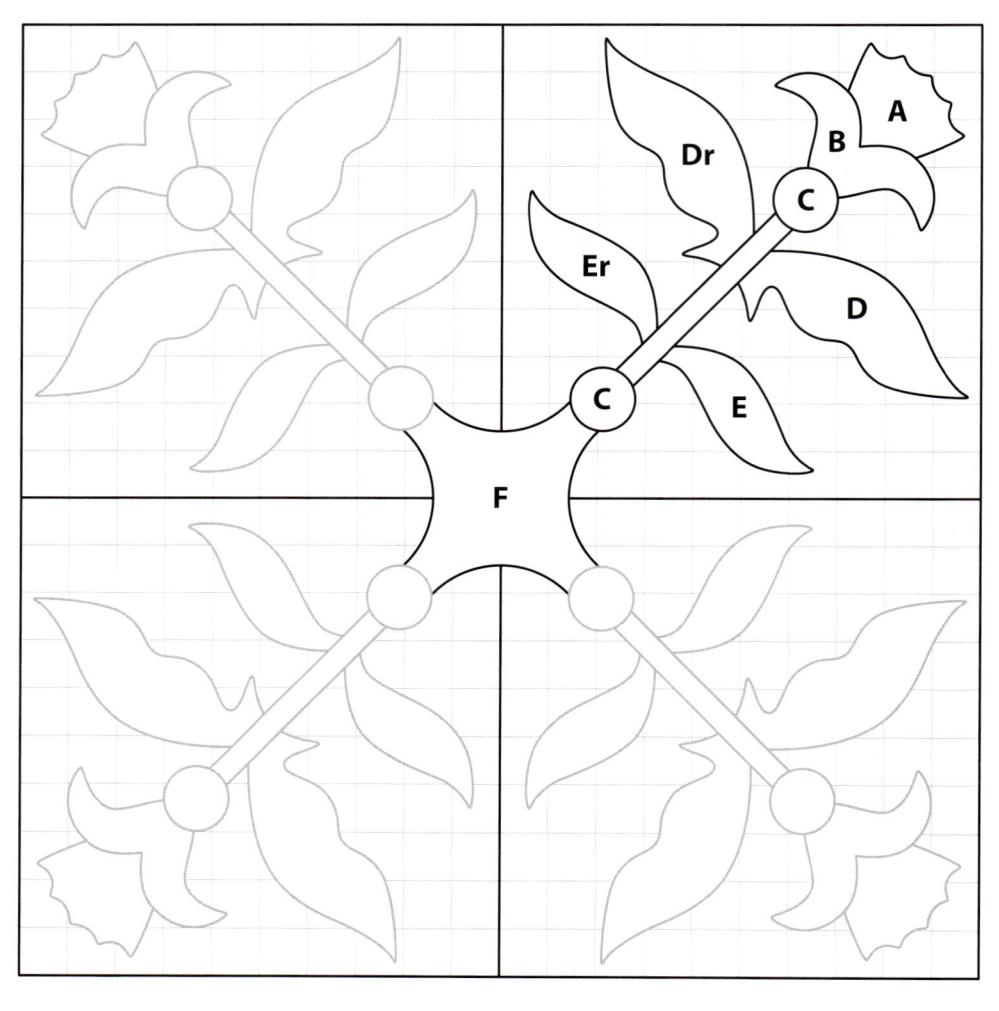

Each square = 1 inch

**A**
Cut 36

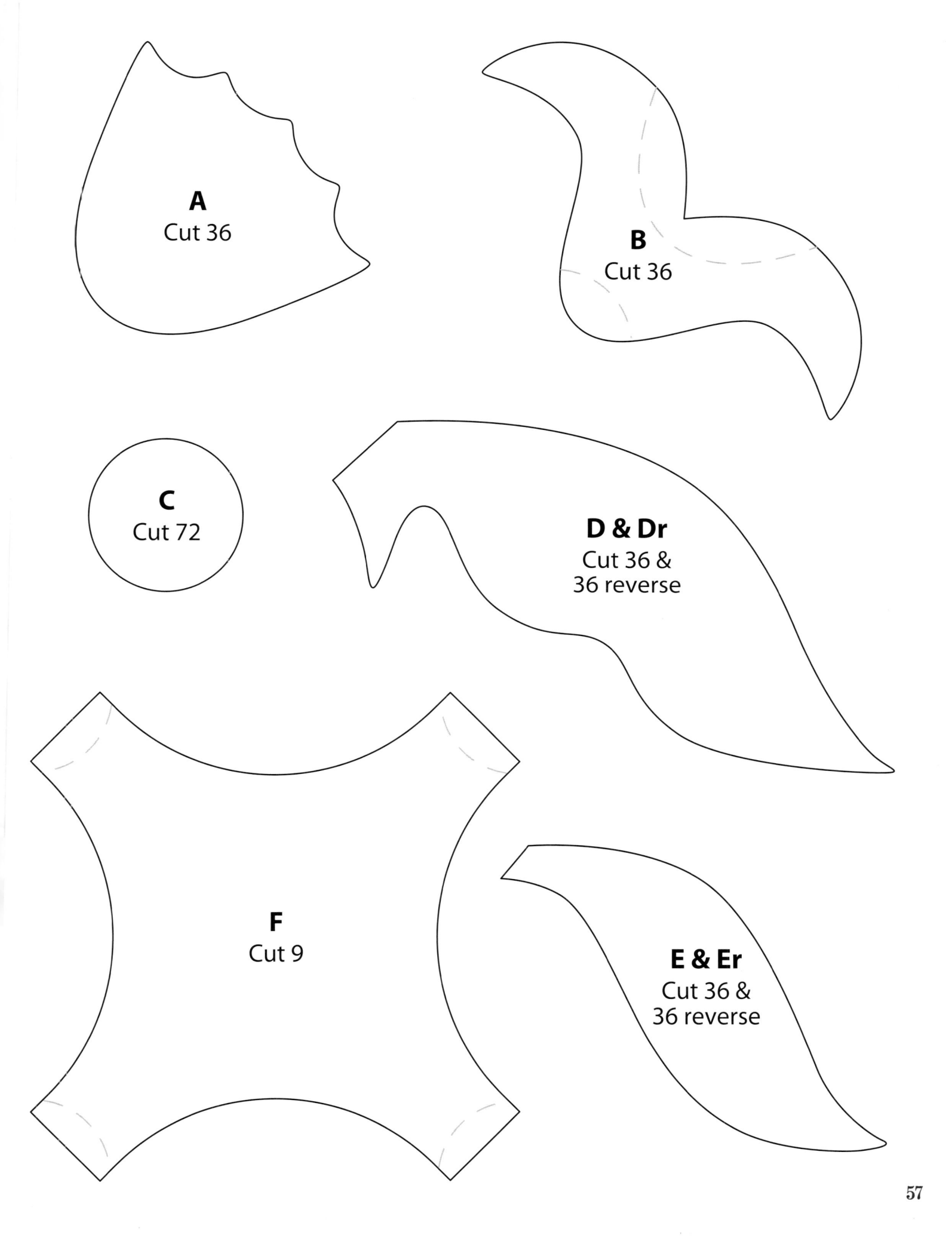

**B**
Cut 36

**C**
Cut 72

**D & Dr**
Cut 36 &
36 reverse

**F**
Cut 9

**E & Er**
Cut 36 &
36 reverse

57

# MY HEART is YOURS

Project Size - 60" x 60"    Finished Block Size - 12"

*Design by* **Barb Adams**
*Appliqué by* **Leona Adams**
*Quilted by* **Jeanne Zyck**

## SUPPLY LIST

- ⅛ yd. each of 8 different red prints
- ⅔ yd. each of 6 different light prints
- ½ yd. for the binding

## INSTRUCTIONS *for* the HEART BLOCK

Cutting measurements include a ¼" seam allowance.

- Cut 4 - 4 ½" squares from a light print. Cut 5 from another light print.

- Find the heart template needed for this block on page 61. Refer to the photo for color placement.

- Cut out 5 heart shapes from the red prints, adding a ⅛" - ¼" seam allowance. Center the heart shape on one light square, and baste it into place.

- Appliqué the heart in place. Repeat for the remaining 4 hearts.

- Refer to the picture of the quilt on page 58. Five heart squares and 4 light fabric squares are sewn together to make one heart block.

- Sew the squares into a block. Repeat for 13 heart blocks. (You will need 117 - 4 ½" squares and 65 hearts to make all of the heart blocks.)

## FINISHING

- Cut 12 - 12 ½" squares from the light prints.
- Refer to the picture on page 58 and sew the quilt top together.

59

60

# MY HEART *is* YOURS TEMPLATE

the house

# SWEET REMEMBRANCE

*Design by* **Barb Adams**
*Stitched by* **Pat Ryan**

## SYMBOLS

x    GA Chamomile (DMC 611)
♥    WDW Lancaster Red (DMC 221)
o    GA Oatmeal (DMC 3865)

GA - Gentle Arts
WDW - Weeks Dye Works

**Design Size:** 47W x 47H
**Fabric:** 30ct. Abecedarian by R & R Reproductions
**Finished Size:** 4" diameter circle

## OTHER SUPPLIES

- 5" square of fabric for backing
- 5" x 10" lightweight fusible interfacing
- ½ yd. beaded trim
- Crushed walnut shells (bird or lizard litter found at pet stores)

## INSTRUCTIONS

- Cross stitch with 2 strands of floss over 2 linen threads.
- Use the alphabet on page 64 to personalize your sampler.
- After the piece is stitched, trace around the circle located on page 64. Use a pencil and plastic template.
- Center the plastic template over the reverse side of the stitched design. Lightly trace the circle onto the linen. Cut out the circle adding a ¼" seam allowance around the circumference.
- Cut 2 pieces of fusible interfacing and backing the same measurement as the linen. Iron one piece of the interfacing onto the reverse side of the backing and the other onto the reverse side the linen.
- Sew the linen front to the fabric backing, right sides together using a ¼" seam allowance. Leave a small opening for turning.
- Turn and stuff with crushed walnut shells. Blind stitch the opening closed.
- Stitch the beaded trim in place along the seam allowance to finish.

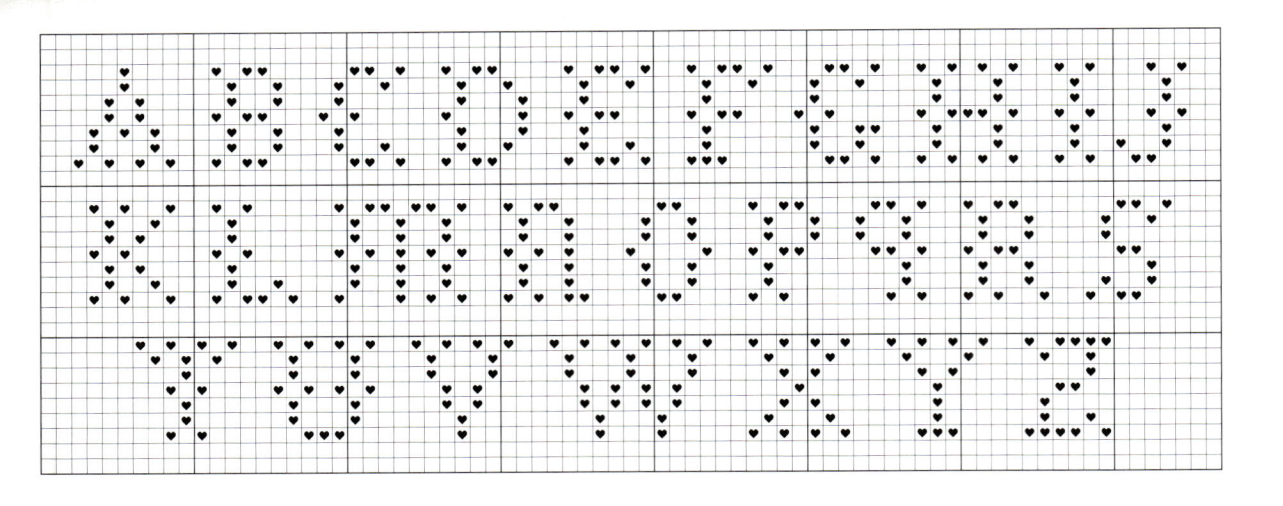

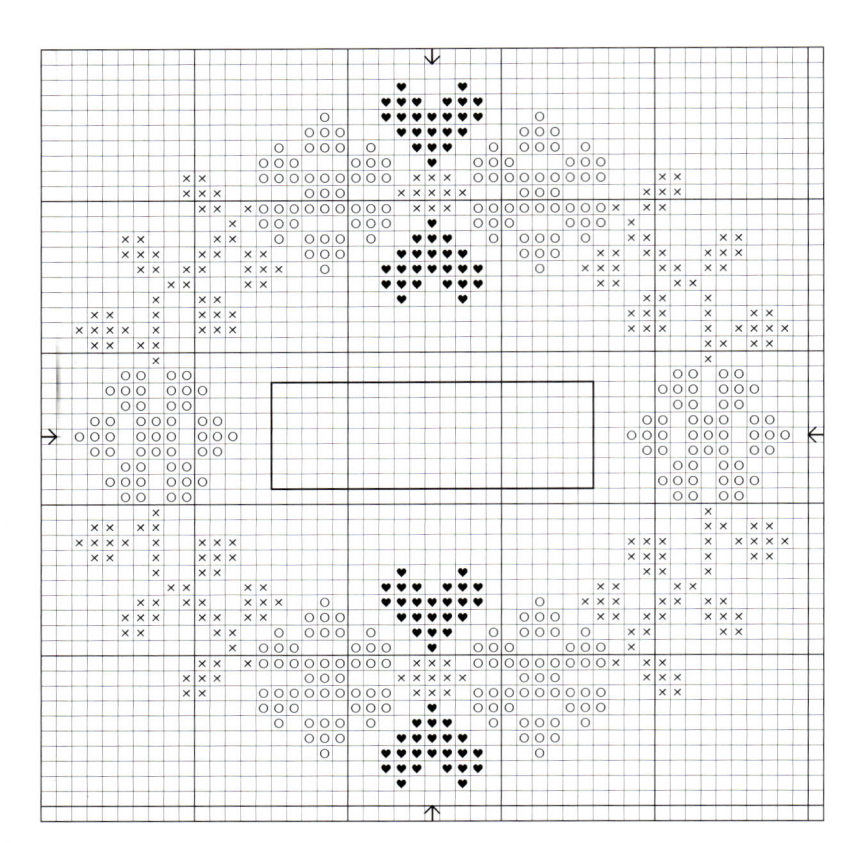

## SYMBOLS

x   GA Chamomile (DMC 611)
♥   WDW Lancaster Red (DMC 221)
o   GA Oatmeal (DMC 3865)

*The symbols are repeated here for your convenience.*

**CIRCLE TEMPLATE**

65

66

# MY GRANDMOTHER'S GARDEN

*Design by* **Alma Allen**
*Stitched by* **Pat Ryan**

## SYMBOLS

- o  GA Antique Rose (DMC 223)
- |  GA Burlap (DMC 437/3771)
- □  CC Bunny Honey (DMC 3771)
- *  GA Carriage Black (DMC 3771/779)
- ●  GA Dried Thyme - 10 yds. (DMC 642)
- ▼  GA Garden Gate (DMC 535)
- \  GA Grasshopper (DMC 372)
- x  GA Toffee (DMC 3829)
- ❤  GA Old Purple Paint (DMC 3860)
- v  CC Old Money (DMC 648/3023)
- -  GA Old Red Paint (DMC 3722)
- +  GA Parchment (DMC 644)
- •  GA Toasted Barley (DMC 3032)

CC - Crescent Colours
GA - Gentle Arts

**Design Size:** 164W x 97H
**Fabric:** 30ct. Mink by R & R Reproductions
**Sampler Size:** 11" x 6 ½"

## INSTRUCTIONS

- Cross stitch with 2 strands of floss over 2 linen threads.
- Stitch the butterfly antenna, thorax and abdomen with one strand of floss. When completed, satin stitch to cover with 2 strands of the same color of floss.
- Stitch the eyelet stitch with 2 strands of Toffee over 4 linen threads. Refer to the illustration below.
- Use the alphabet provided to replace the name and date with your own.

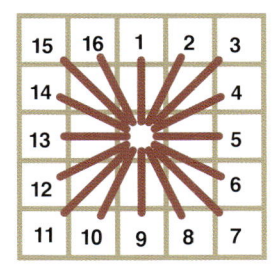

Eyelet stitch over
4 linen threads

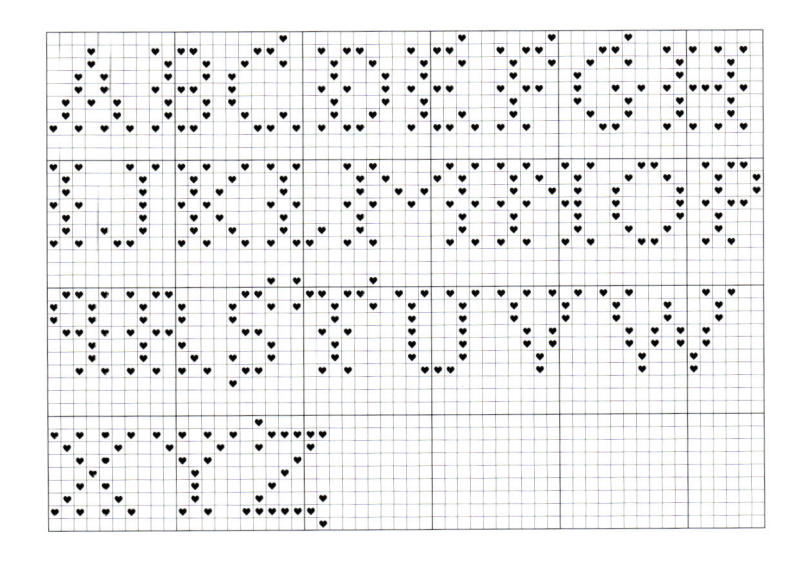

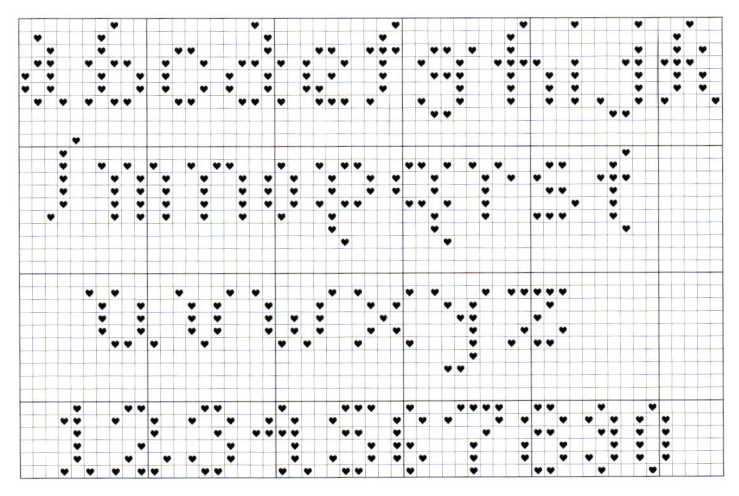

## SYMBOLS

- ○ GA Antique Rose (DMC 223)
- | GA Burlap (DMC 437/3771)
- □ CC Bunny Honey (DMC 3771)
- ▼ GA Carriage Black (DMC 3771/779)
- ● GA Dried Thyme - 10 yds. (DMC 642)
- ✸ GA Garden Gate (DMC 535)
- \ GA Grasshopper (DMC 372)

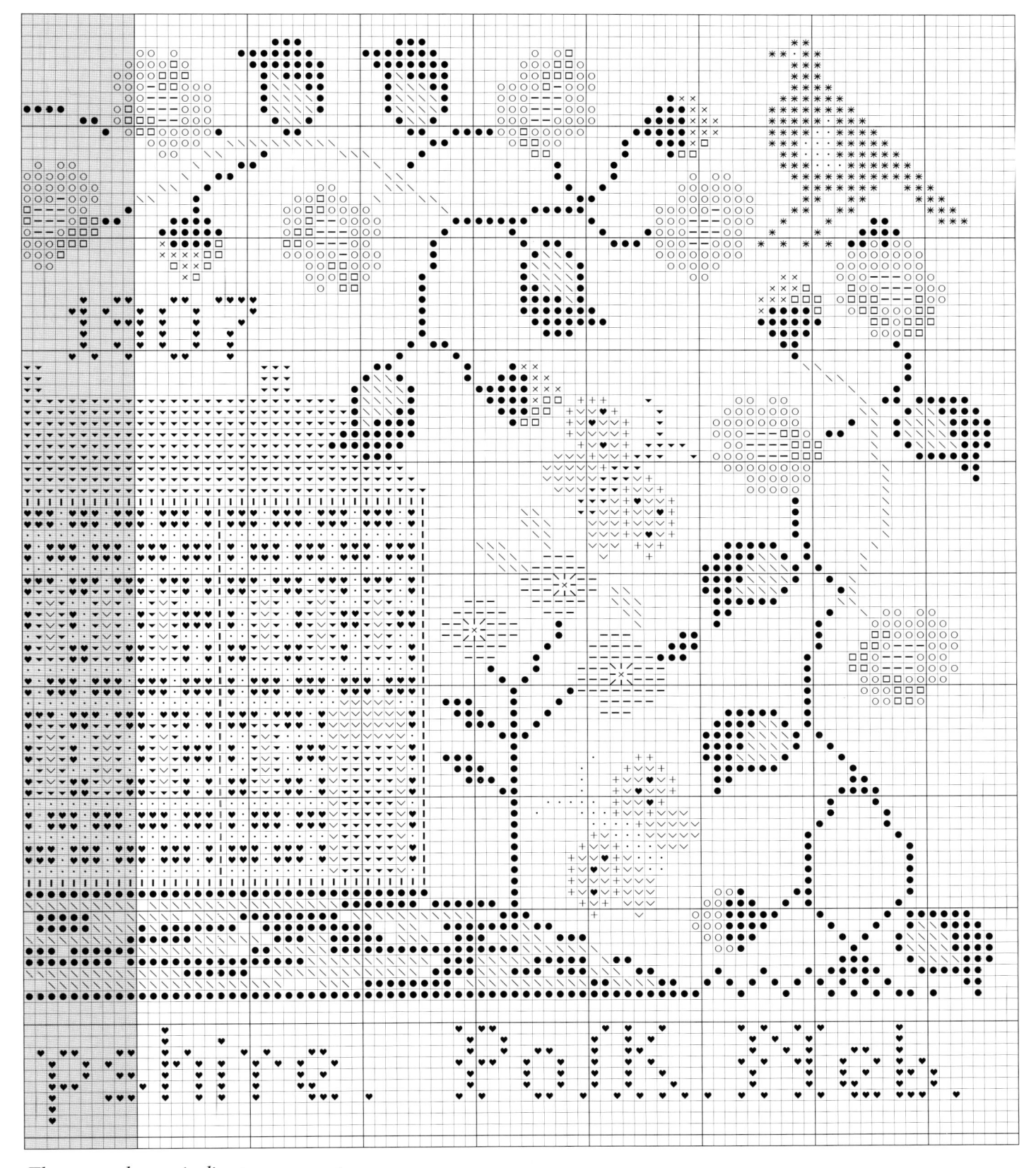

The grayed area indicates a repeat.

x  GA Toffee (DMC 3829)

♥  GA Old Purple Paint (DMC 3860)

v  CC Old Money (DMC 648/3023)

-  GA Old Red Paint (DMC 3722)

+  GA Parchment (DMC 644)

•  GA Toasted Barley (DMC 3032)

*The symbols are repeated here for your convenience.*

70

# HOOKED RUG

*Design by* Alma Allen
*Hooked by* Sandy Williams *of American Whatever*

## SUPPLY LIST

### Wool

- 1 ¼ yds. of fudge brown for the background

**Flowers:**

- 3" x 8" light yellow plaid for the flower centers
- 6" x 28" dark pink
- 6" x 28" medium pink
- 6" x 28" light pink

**Grass, leaves and stems:** (blend the three for the grass)

- 9" x 27" light green
- 14" x 28" medium green
- 5" x 30" another medium green

**House:**

- 8" x 27" light blue/gray spot dye for the roof and windows
- 1" x 16" different blue for the door
- 3" x 16" light for the inside of the windows
- 4" x 28" light shade for the right side of the house
- 7" x 28" medium light shade for the left side of the house
- 1" x 16" gray for the chimneys

**Butterflies:**

- 2 ½" x 28" light lavender gray for the thorax
- 5" x 25" lavender tweed for the upper wing
- 3" x 25" light plaid for the butterfly outline
- 3" x 16" rosy lavender check for the bottom wing

### Other Supplies

- Red dot tracer or nylon organdy
- ¾ yd. monk's cloth or rug linen
- Sharpie permanent marker
- Dark brown and green yarn for binding
- 3 ¾ yds. binding tape for finishing

**Project Size - 35" x 19 ¾"**

**American Whatever -**
**Wool and hooking supplies**
(816) 781-3244
131 South Water Street
Liberty, MO 64068

# INSTRUCTIONS

- Sew around the edge of the rug linen using a zig-zag stitch to prevent fraying.

- Center and draw the design on red dot tracer or nylon organdy. Center the red dot tracer or nylon organdy on the linen. Retrace the design with a Sharpie permanent marker. The ink from the marker will bleed through the red dot tracer onto the rug linen.

- Use a #8 blade cut on your wool strips.

- Outline and hook the shapes first.

- After the shapes are filled, begin hooking the background following the contours of the pattern. First, for a smooth appearance, outline the shapes with the background color. Continue to outline the shapes until the outlines begin to meet. Fill the spaces remaining, following a natural flow of hooking.

## FINISHING TECHNIQUES

- Place the finished rug face down on a dampened towel, and press using a medium setting on the steam iron.

- Bind the edges with dark brown yarn. Use a green yarn to bind the grass area.

- Trim the edges to ½" and sew twill tape over the raw edges.

Each square = 1"
Enlarge diagram 357%

73

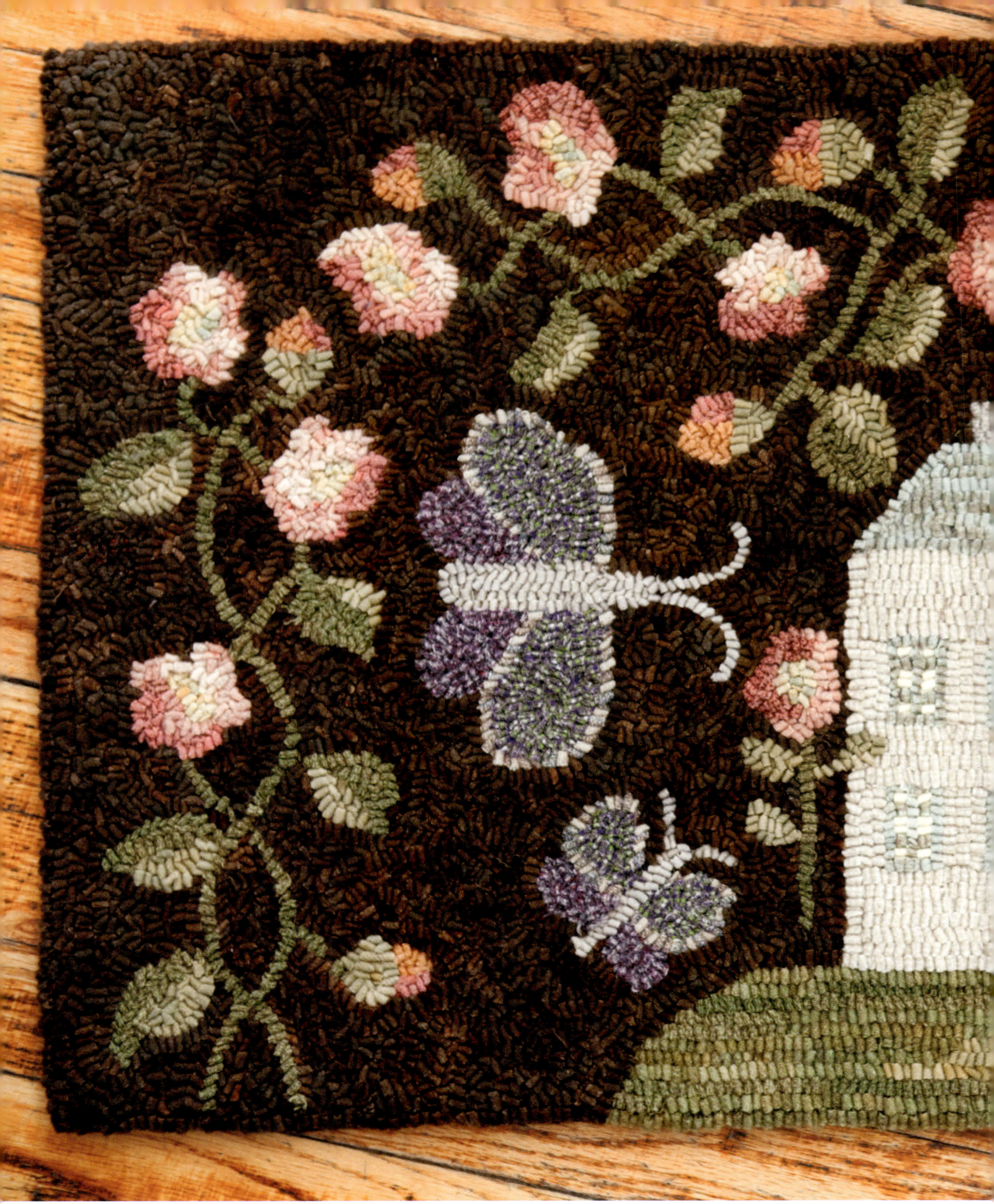

75

# SHAKER SEWING BOX

*Design by Alma Allen*
*Hooked by Alma Allen*

Project Size - 8" diameter

## SUPPLY LIST

### Wool
- 8" x 27" cocoa brown for the background

### Flowers:
- 3" x 27" light apricot for the flowers
- 2" x 27" light pink for the flowers
- ½" x 27" darker pink for the flowers
- 2" x 27" antique white for the flower centers

### Stems and leaves:
- 2" x 27" light blue for the leaves
- 3" x 27" sage green for the leaves and stems

### Basket:
- 3" x 27" pale gold for the basket

### Other Supplies:
- ½ yd. batting
- Fat quarter of a coordinating fabric
- Piece of cardboard

8" Sewing box: Lone Elm Lane - Early Wooden Wares
loneelmlane@comcast.net
www.loneelmlane.com
(913)980-3666

## HOOKING INSTRUCTIONS

- Sew around the edge of the rug linen using a zig-zag stitch to prevent fraying.

- Center and draw the design on red dot tracer or nylon organdy. Center the red dot tracer or nylon organdy on the linen. Retrace the design with a Sharpie permanent marker. The ink from the marker will bleed through the red dot tracer onto the rug linen.

- Use a #4 blade cut on your wool strips.

- Outline and hook the shapes first.

- After the shapes are filled, begin hooking the background following the contours of the pattern. First, for a smooth appearance, outline the shapes with the background color. Continue to outline the shapes until the outlines begin to meet. Fill the spaces remaining, following a natural flow of hooking.

## FINISHING TECHNIQUES

- Place the finished rug face down on a dampened towel, and press using a medium setting on the steam iron.

- Use the wooden circle insert provided in the box as a template and trim your canvas, adding a 2 ½" border around the circumference.

- Cut 1 piece of cardboard and 2 pieces of batting the same size as the circle template.

- Position the cardboard circle and layers of batting on top of the circle template. Center the hooked piece on top and lace them all together.

- Push the stitched piece into the top of the box.

77

78

# WOODEN SEWING BOX HOOKED RUG PATTERN

Each square = 1 inch

80

# GARDEN HOUSE TABLE or BED RUNNER

*Design by* **Barb Adams**
*Sewing and Quilting by* **Jeanne Zyck**

**Project Size - 24" x 60"**

## SUPPLY LIST

The fabric numbers are from the collection of **Cinnamon Spice** by Blackbird Designs for Moda Fabrics.

**For the background:**
- 1 yd. each of 2 tan prints for backgrounds and pieced blocks (2702-24 & 2701-24)
- ¼ yd. of another tan print

**For the appliqué and pieced blocks:**
- 1 yd. of a red floral print - includes the binding (2700-22)
- ½ yd. each of a red print (2706-12) and a red plaid
- ½ yd. of a brown and taupe plaid
- ¼ yd. each of 3 different brown and taupe prints and stripes
- ¼" and ½" Clover bias tape makers

## INSTRUCTIONS for the BASKET BLOCK

- Cut a 16 ½" x 12 ½" rectangle from light fabric for the background of the basket block.
- Make 1 ¼ yds. of ¼" bias tape for the stems.
- The templates are located on pages 85 - 86. Cut out the shapes, adding a ⅛" - ¼" seam allowance. Refer to the diagram on page 85, and baste the pieces in place on the background block.
- Appliqué the pieces in place. Set the block aside.

## INSTRUCTIONS for the HOUSE BLOCK

- Cut a 24 ½" x 20 ½" rectangle from light fabric for the background of the house block.
- Cut a 20" x 14 ¼" rectangle from a red plaid for the house.
- Make 1 ⅓ yds. of ½" bias tape for the tree branches.
- Make 30" of ¼" bias tape for the window panes.
- The templates are located on pages 87 - 89. Cut out the shapes, adding a ⅛" - ¼" seam allowance. Refer to the diagram on page 87, and baste the pieces in place on the background block.
- Appliqué the pieces in place. Set the block aside.

## INSTRUCTIONS for the VINE BLOCK

- Cut a 16 ½" x 10 ½" rectangle from light fabric for the background of the vine block.
- Make 1 yd. of ½" bias tape for the vine.
- Make 10" of ¼" bias tape for the berry stems.
- The templates are located on page 91. Cut out the shapes, adding a ⅛" - ¼" seam allowance. Refer to the diagram on page 90, and baste the pieces in place on the background block.
- Appliqué the pieces in place. Set the block aside.

*Instructions continue on the following page.*

# INSTRUCTIONS *for the* TWO 8" STAR BLOCKS

- Cut 2 - 4 ½" squares, one from a red print and one from a brown print. Set these aside. Refer to the picture of the two 8" star blocks on the right. Make the star block on the right first.

- Cut 4 - 2 ⅞ " squares from a red print.

- Cut 1 - 5 ½" square from a tan print.

- Draw a diagonal line on the reverse side of each red square.

- Align 2 red squares on top of the 5 ½" tan square, right sides together, as shown in the illustration.

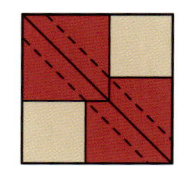

- Sew a scant ¼" seam on each side of the drawn line.

- Cut apart on the drawn line and press toward the red triangles.

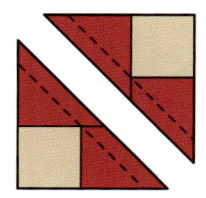

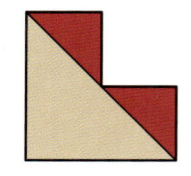

- Align another red square on the tan triangle as shown in the illustration below. Again, sew a scant ¼" seam on each side of the drawn line. Cut the pieces apart on the drawn line, and press toward the red triangles. Repeat for the remaining unit. The results will be four flying geese units.

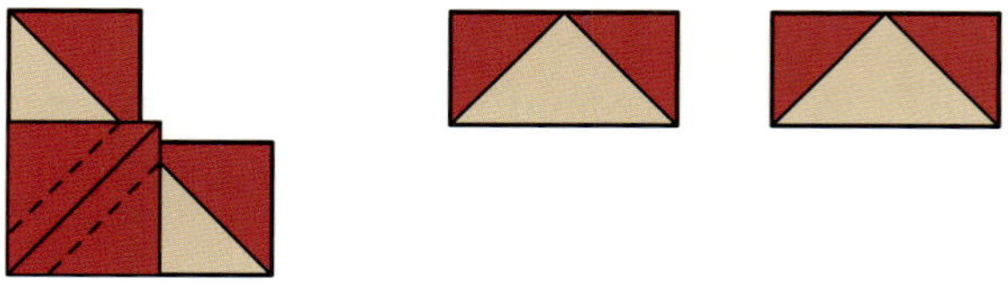

- Cut 4 - 2 ½" squares from a tan print. Sew one to each end of a flying geese unit. Make 2. Refer to the star block sewing guide.

- Sew a flying geese unit to either side of the 4 ½" brown center square.

- Refer to the Star block sewing guide and sew the three units together to complete the block.

**The two 8" star blocks**

**Star block sewing diagram**

- Repeat the method described earlier for making the flying geese blocks using 4 - 2 ⅞" taupe squares and a 5 ½" tan print square.

- Cut 4 – 2 ½" squares from a tan print. Sew one to each end of a flying geese unit. Make 2. Refer to the star block sewing diagram.

- Sew a flying geese unit to either side of the 4 ½" red center square.

- Refer to the star block sewing guide and sew the three units together to complete the block.

- Refer to the picture above of the two 8" star blocks, and sew the two star blocks together.

- Refer to the picture on pages 90 - 91, and sew the 2-star block unit onto the top of the basket block. Sew this unit onto the right side of the house block unit.

82

## INSTRUCTIONS for the LARGE 10" STAR BLOCK

- Cut 1 - 5 ½" square from a red print. Set it aside.
- Cut 4 - 3 ⅜" squares from a brown/taupe print.
- Cut 1 - 6 ¼" square from a tan print.
- Draw a diagonal line on the reverse side of each brown/taupe square.
- Align 2 brown/taupe squares on top of the 6 ¼" tan square, right sides together, as shown in the illustration on page 82.
- Sew a scant ¼" seam on each side of the drawn line.
- Cut apart on the drawn line and press toward the brown/taupe triangles.
- Align another brown/taupe square on the tan triangle as shown in the illustration on page 82. Again, sew a scant ¼" seam on each side of the drawn line. Cut the pieces apart on the drawn line, and press toward the brown/taupe triangles. Repeat for the remaining unit. The results will be four flying geese units.
- Cut 4 - 3" squares from a tan print. Sew one to each end of a flying geese unit. Make 2. Refer to the star block sewing diagram on page 82.
- Sew a flying geese unit to either side of the 5 ½" red center square.
- Refer to the star block sewing guide on page 82, and sew the three units together to complete the block.

## INSTRUCTIONS for the TWO 4-PATCH BLOCKS

- Cut 4 - 3 ½" x 3" rectangles from a mixture of red prints.
- Cut 4 - 3 ½" x 3" rectangles from a tan print.
- Refer to the illustration to the right and make two 4-patch blocks. They will measure 5 ½" x 6 ½" unfinished. Sew the two blocks together. Refer to the picture on pages 90 - 91, and sew the blocks to the right side of the large star block to form a unit.

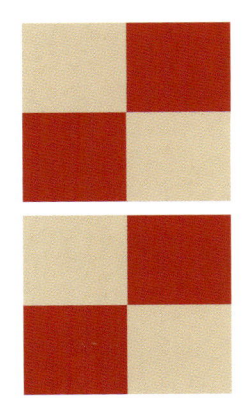

- Refer to the picture on pages 90 - 91, and sew the star unit onto the bottom of the vine block.
- Refer to the picture on pages 90 - 91, and sew the vine unit onto the left side of the house block.

## INSTRUCTIONS for the FLYING GEESE BORDER

- Cut 84 - 2 ⅞" squares from a mixture of red prints.
- Cut 42 - 5 ½" squares from a mixture of tan prints.
- Repeat the method described earlier for making the flying geese blocks and make 42 units.
- Sew 2 strips of 6 units each. Refer to the illustration below and align one strip on a side of the table runner. Sew into place. Trim away the excess on both sides. Repeat for the opposite side.

- Sew 2 strips of 15 units each. Sew one to the top and one to the bottom of the piece to finish the runner.

83

84

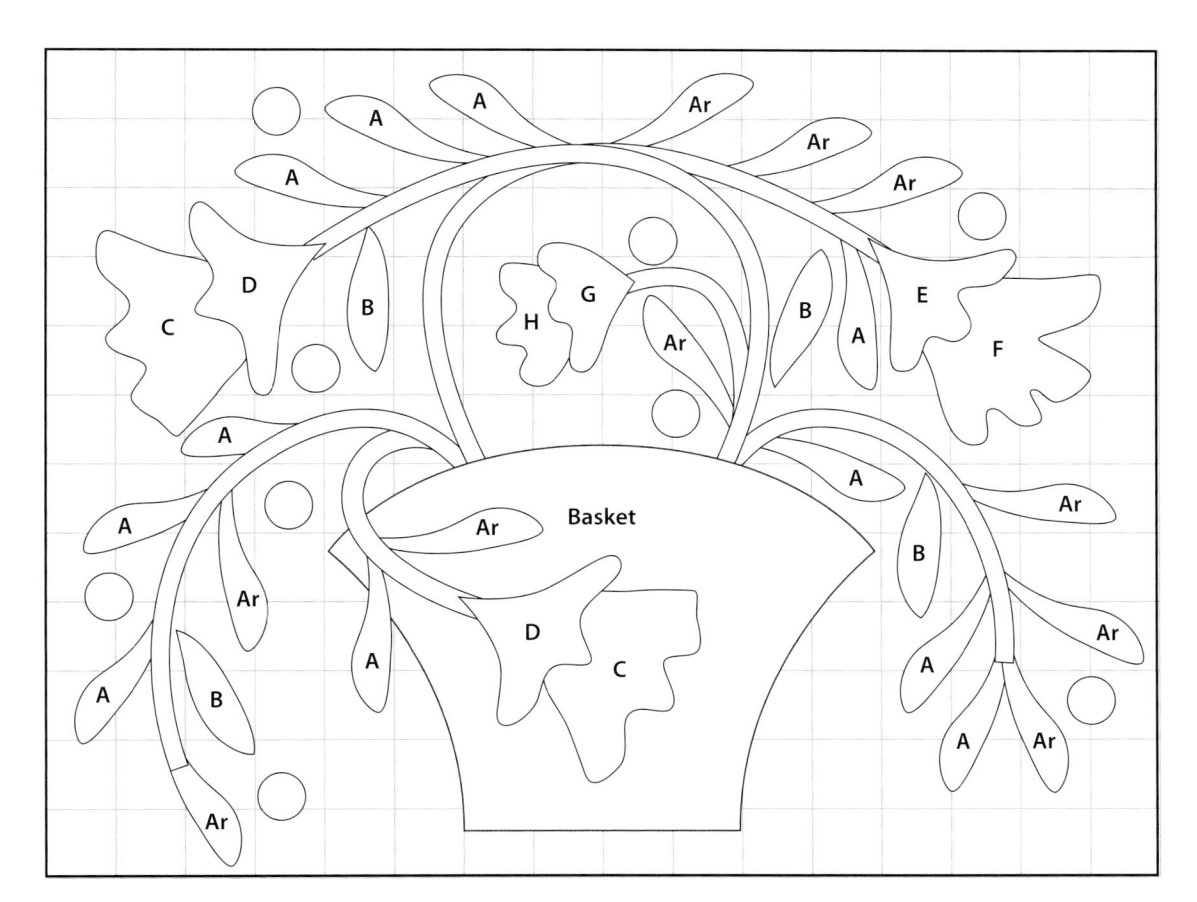

Each square = 1 inch

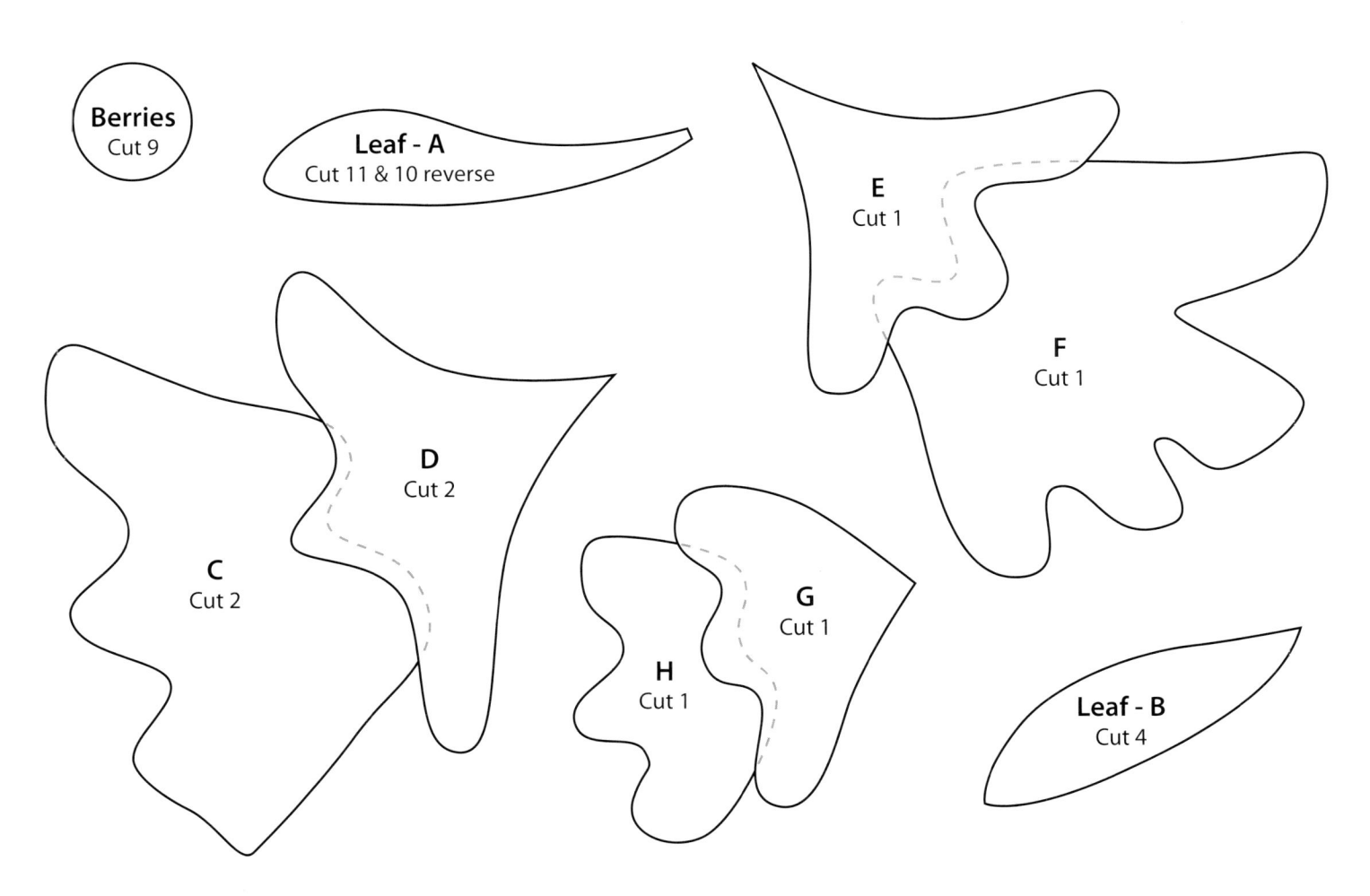

**Berries** Cut 9

**Leaf - A** Cut 11 & 10 reverse

**C** Cut 2

**D** Cut 2

**E** Cut 1

**F** Cut 1

**H** Cut 1

**G** Cut 1

**Leaf - B** Cut 4

85

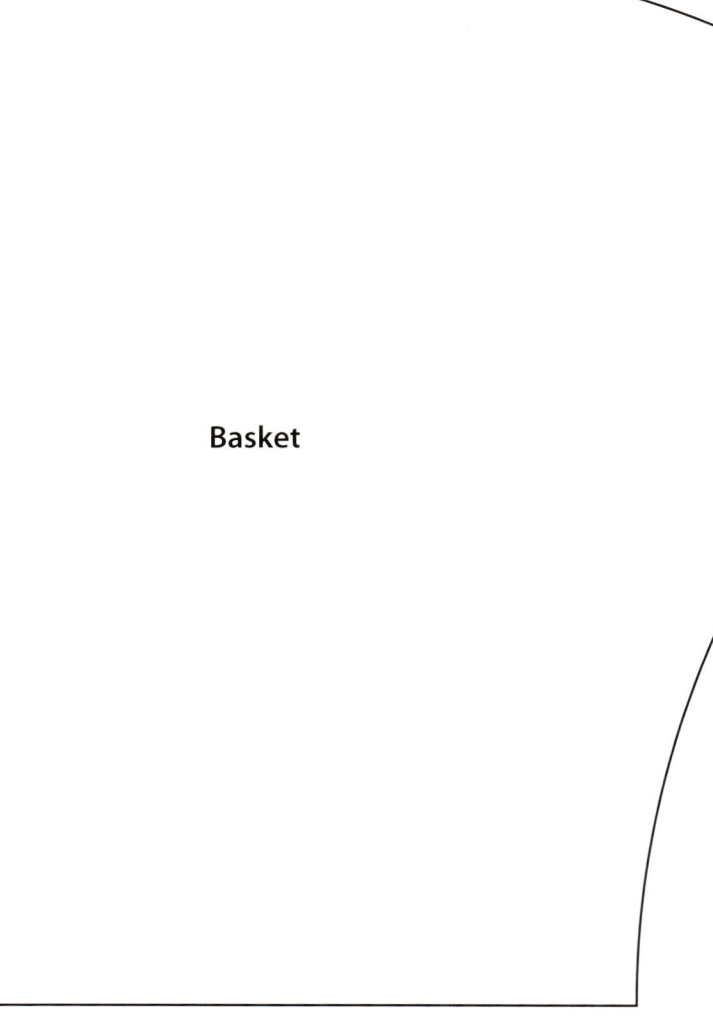

Basket

86

Each square = 1 inch

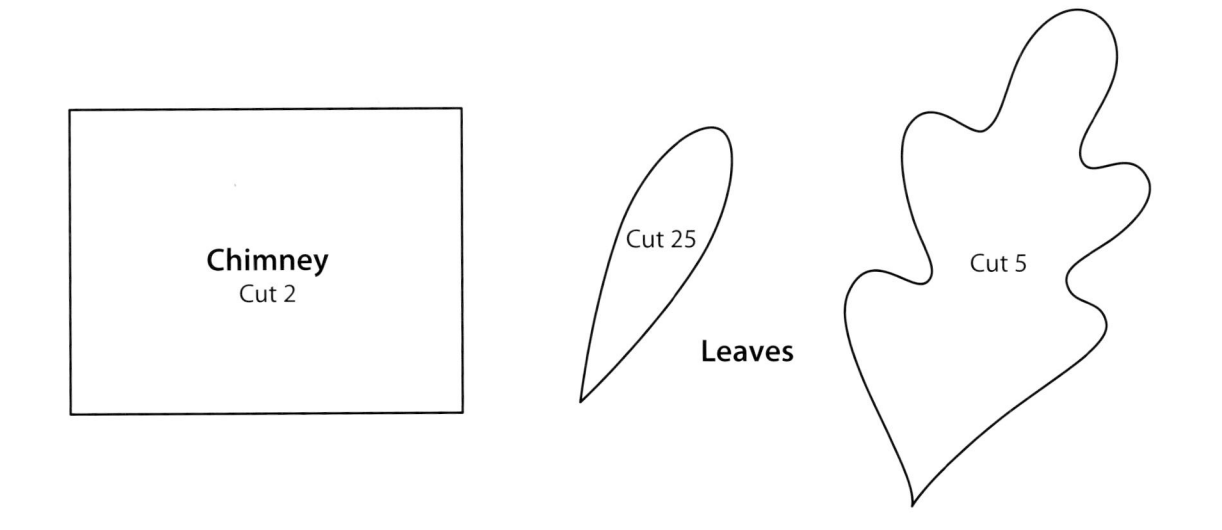

**Chimney**
Cut 2

**Leaves**
Cut 25

Cut 5

87

**Window** - Cut 5

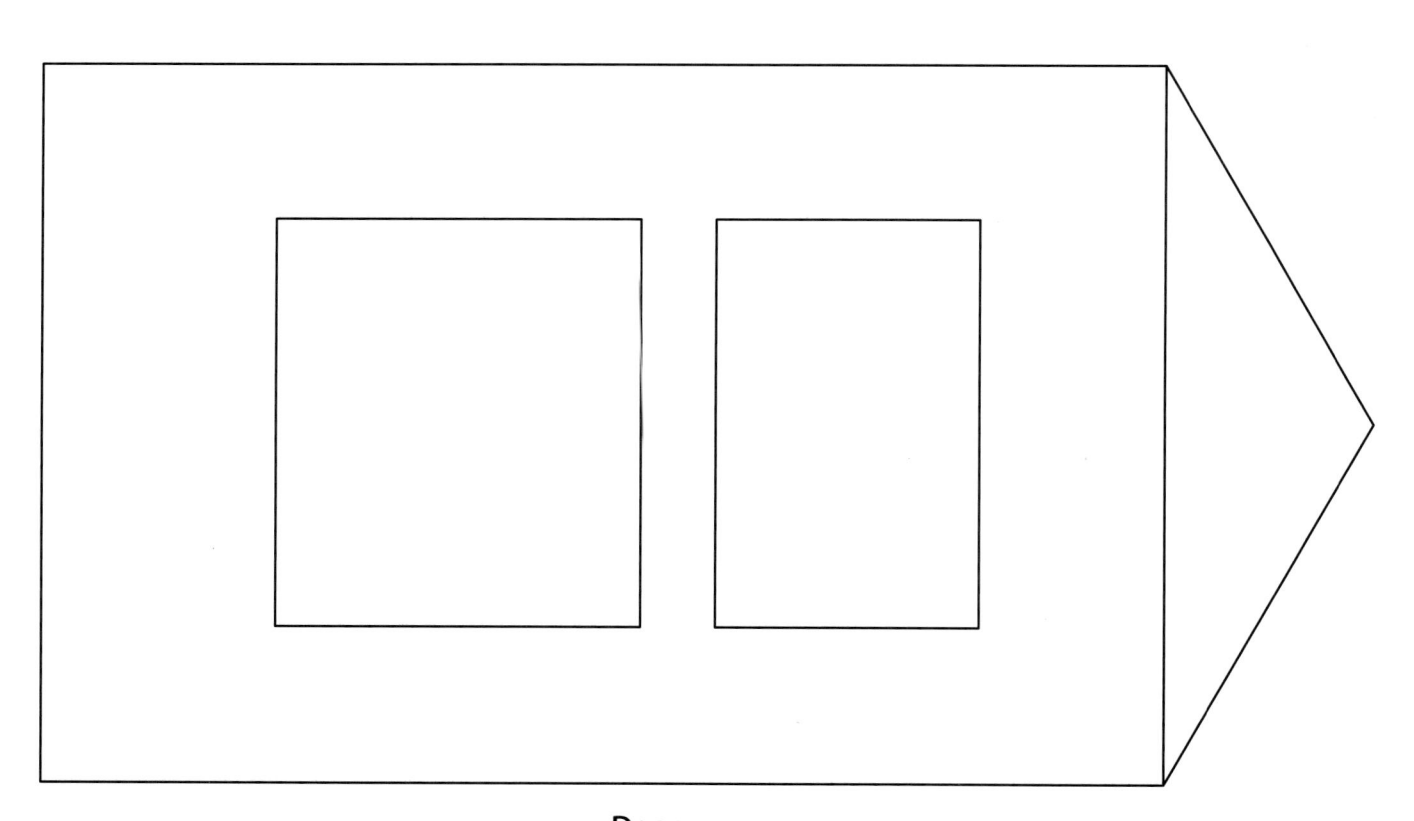

**Door**

88

Roof

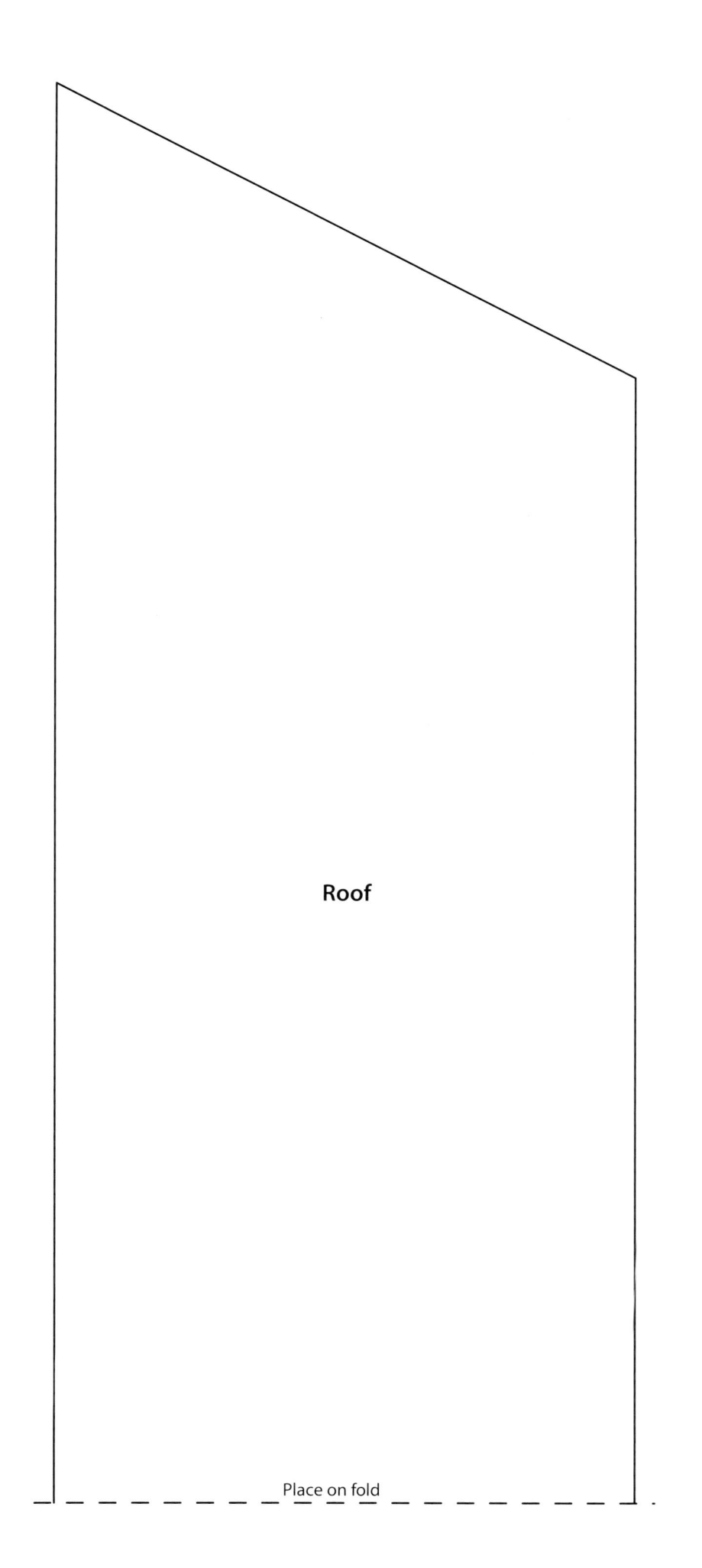

Place on fold

Leaf A

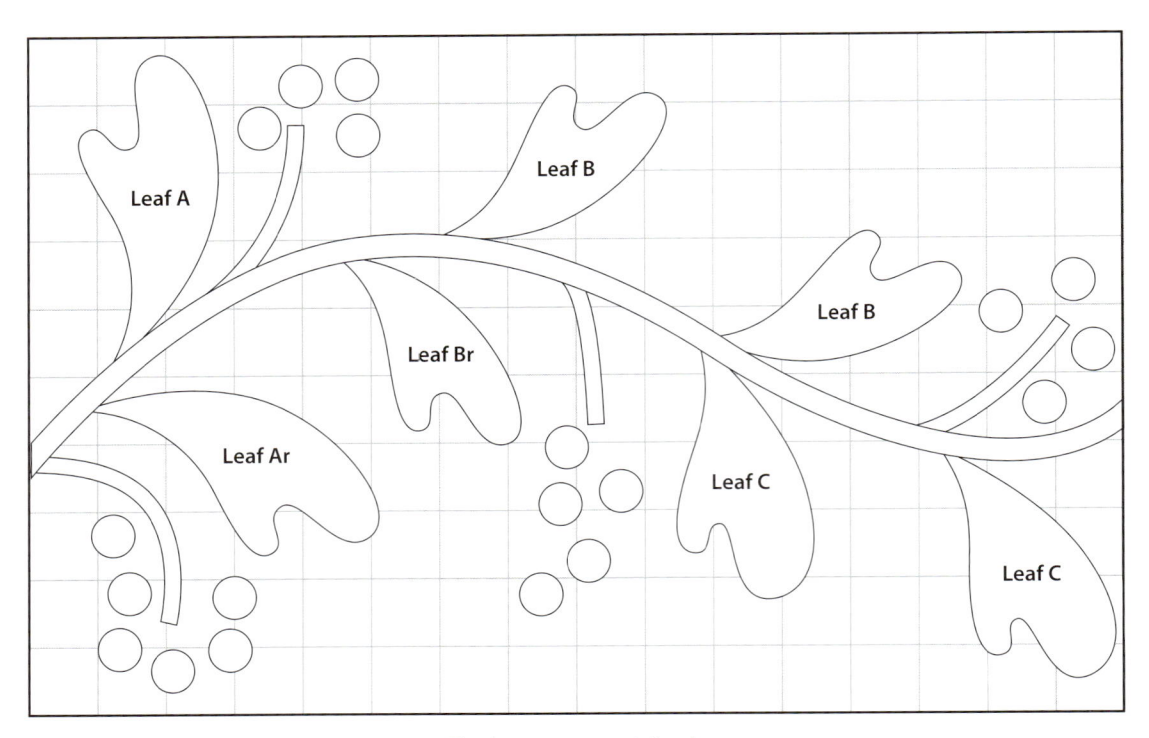

Leaf B

Leaf Br

Leaf Ar

Leaf B

Leaf C

Leaf C

Each square = 1 inch

90

Cut 19  Berries

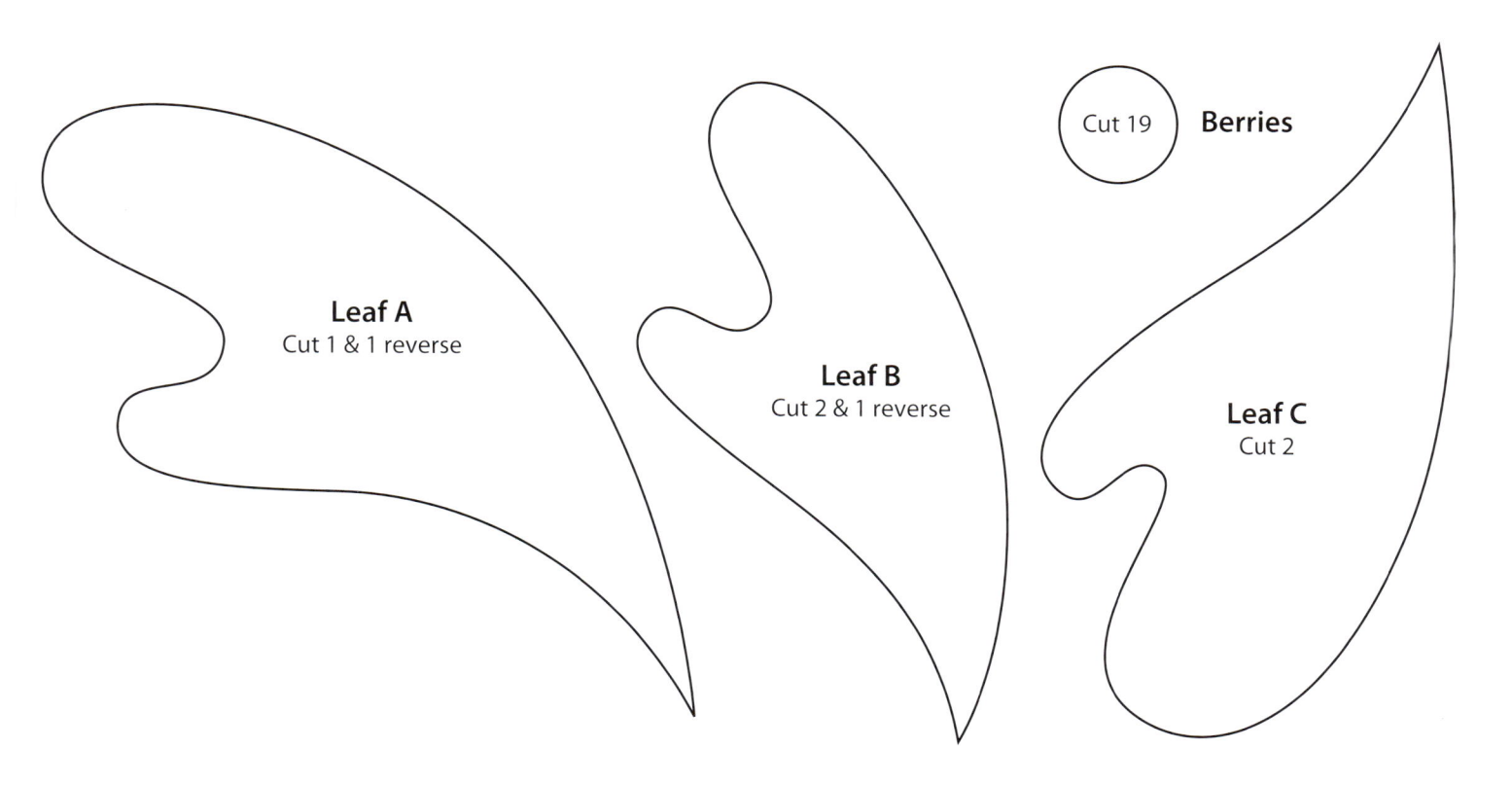

**Leaf A**
Cut 1 & 1 reverse

**Leaf B**
Cut 2 & 1 reverse

**Leaf C**
Cut 2

91

92

# VINTAGE BLANKET

*Project by* **Barb Adams**

**Project Size - Full bed size**

## SUPPLY LIST

- Vintage crocheted tablecloth
- 3 bottles of Rit dye - Kelly Green
- 1 bottle of Rit dye - Black
- 1 cup of salt

Barb has found some great antique crocheted tablecloths and coverlets at estate sales. Many still have all of their stitches intact yet have discolorations that make them hard to display. Refresh these wonderful textiles with a bit of dye. They are great on the bed as a blanket or on the table adding a dramatic bold color.

## DYEING INSTRUCTIONS

- Follow the dye instructions using cold water in the washing machine.

- Place the coverlet in the washer on a rinse cycle to completely wet the crochet cotton. After the rinse cycle is complete, remove the wet coverlet and set it aside.

- Fill the washer with cold water on the longest wash cycle. Add the bottles of dye and salt. Allow the washer to agitate the dye mix to blend the colors and salt for a minute. Place the machine on pause and add the wet coverlet. Complete the wash and rinse cycle. Add another rinse cycle to remove the extra dye that has not been absorbed.

- Check the wet coverlet for the desired color. The coverlet will be a lighter shade when it has dried.

- Dry the coverlet on a low setting in the dryer. Remove the coverlet while it is still damp, and lay it flat to finish drying.

# SUMMER STARS

Project Size - 80" x 80"   Finished Block Size - 8"

*Design by* Barb Adams
*Sewing by* Leona Adams
*Quilting by* Jeanne Zyck

## SUPPLY LIST

The fabric numbers are from the collection of **Cinnamon Spice** by Blackbird Designs for Moda Fabrics.

- 1 ½ yds. of a red floral print (2700-22)
- 2 ½ yds. of a red print - includes binding (2706-12)
- 1 ⅓ yds. each of 5 different tan prints (2706-14, 2704-24, 2702-14, 2703-14 and one additional print)

## INSTRUCTIONS

Cutting measurements include a ¼" seam allowance.

- Cut 40 - 8 ½" squares from the tan prints for the alternating blocks. Set these aside.

**For each star block:**

- Cut 1 - 4 ½" square from one of the red prints. Set aside.
- Cut 1 - 5 ½" square from a tan print.
- Cut 4 - 2 ⅞" squares from a red print.
- Draw a diagonal line on the reverse side of each 2 ⅞" red square.
- Align 2 red squares on top of the 5 ½" tan square, right sides together, as shown in the illustration.

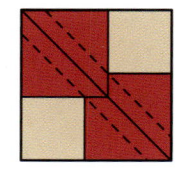

- Sew a scant ¼" seam on each side of the drawn line.

- Cut apart on the drawn line, and press toward the red triangles.

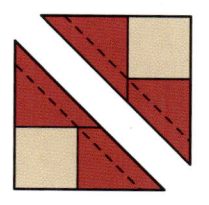

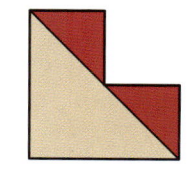

- Align another red square on the tan triangle as shown in the illustration. Again, sew a scant ¼" seam on each side of the drawn line. Cut the pieces apart on the drawn line, and press toward the red triangles. Repeat for the remaining unit. The results will be four flying geese units.

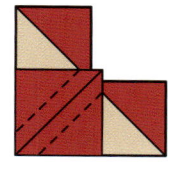

- Cut 4 – 2 ½" squares from a tan print. Sew one to each end of a flying geese unit. Make 2. Refer to the Star block sewing guide.
- Sew a flying geese unit to either side of the 4 ½" center square.
- Refer to the star block sewing guide and sew the three units together to complete the block. Make 41 star blocks.
- Refer to the picture on page 94, and sew the star and alternating blocks together.

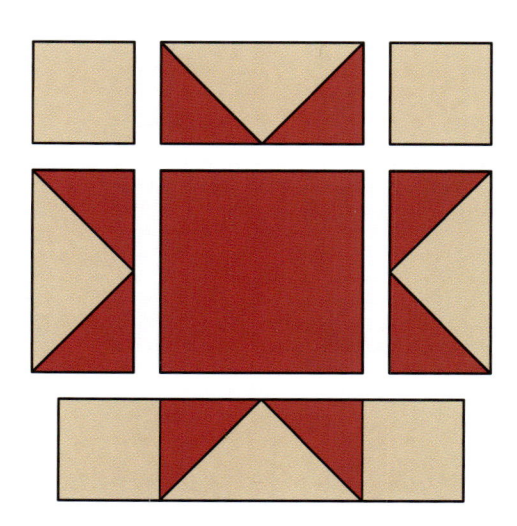

**Star block sewing guide**

95

# BORDER INSTRUCTIONS

- Cut 8 - 9 ¼" squares from a mix of the two red prints. Cut each square on the diagonal twice.

- Cut 9 - 9 ¼" squares from a mix of the tan prints. Cut each square on the diagonal twice.

- Cut 2 - 8 ⅞" squares from a red print. Cut each square once on the diagonal for the corners. Set these aside.

- Refer to the illustration showing how to align the triangles for sewing, and sew a strip of 8 red triangles and 9 tan triangles. Repeat for 4 strips. Sew one strip to each side of the quilt top.

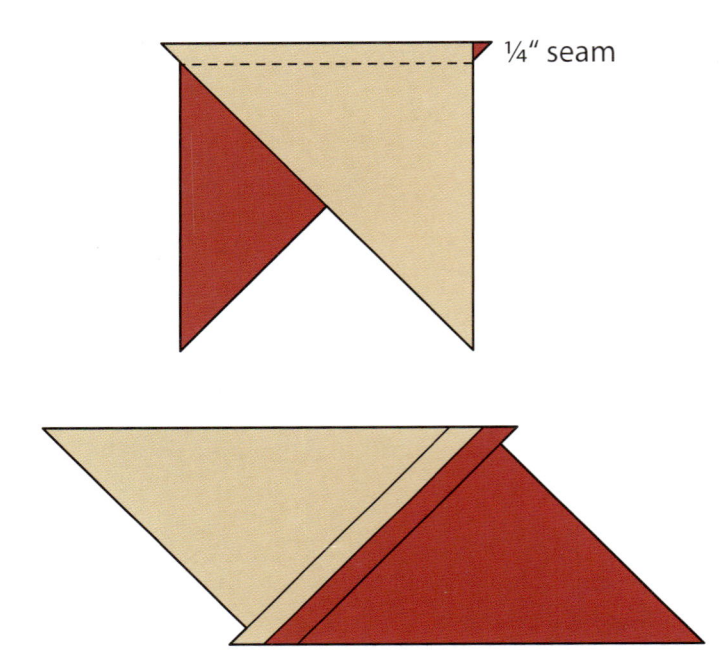

- Refer to the sewing illustration, and sew a large triangle to each corner of the quilt top to finish.

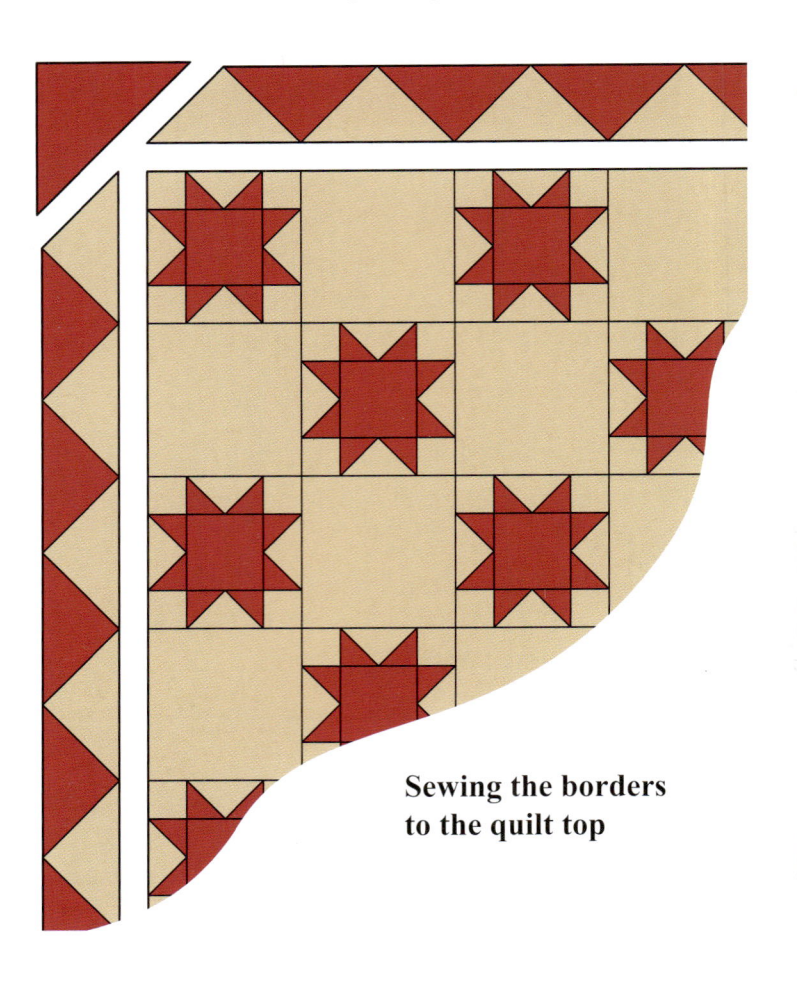

¼" seam

**Sewing the borders to the quilt top**

96